WOOD CARVING

WOOD CARVING is one of the oldest crafts, and this book deals with all aspects of the subject in a modern way, so that the beginner can learn the elementary steps and follow his own interests as his skill develops. The keen craftsman who is already a woodworker will find that carving gives him an opportunity of putting an individual finish on the things he makes, while any man or woman looking for a means of developing their artistic expression in a traditionally sound way will find that wood carving has much to offer them.

WOOD CARVING

by

PERCY W. BLANDFORD

W. & G. FOYLE LTD
119-125 CHARING CROSS ROAD
LONDON W.C.2

© *W. & G. Foyle Ltd.* 1959
Reprinted November 1969
Revised Edition 1972
Reprinted 1973
Reprinted April 1974

Printed in Great Britain by
REDWOOD BURN LIMITED
Trowbridge & Esher

CONTENTS

PREFACE

Wood carving is almost certainly the oldest of the arts. The earliest craftsman whittled wood with his primitive tools, and carving has continued through the centuries to the present day. It is fitting that we as twentieth century wood carvers should keep alive this ancient craft.

Wood carving is both an art and a craft. The carver who is primarily an artist, will get ample opportunities of expressing himself while fashioning objects in the round, but the carver who is more interested in craftsmanship will get his reward from the skilful execution of a leaf or scroll. Both will feel the immense satisfaction of carrying an original job through to its conclusion—a rarity in this highly specialised industrial age.

Wood carving need not be expensive. The essential tools are comparatively few, and much can be done with half-a-dozen gouges. Providing the right wood and designs are chosen, no great strength is needed and carving may be done by women as well as men. The man who is already an amateur or professional woodworker, will find in carving, a further means of using his skill and interest in wood to make his products more complete.

There are many aspects of carving—simple incisions, low or deep relief work, chip carving, sculpture and combined carving and turning. Each carver will find the one which best suits his skill and temperament, but an occasional excursion into the other branches will provide interest and enlarge his scope. There is no other modern book covering all aspects of wood carving, and it is hoped that this little book will satisfy a need.

I should like to thank William Marples & Sons Ltd. of Sheffield for providing details of standard sizes and shapes of carving tools, and the following two firms for providing details of the combination tools which they supply: Phillips Omnipool Ltd., 406 Euston Rd., London, N.W.1; Trix Ltd., Old Burlington St., London, W.1.

P. W. Blandford

CHAPTER I

TOOLS AND MATERIALS

CARVING tools are made in a bewildering range of shapes and sizes, and the beginner may be forgiven if he wonders whether he can afford to take up carving. Fortunately quite a small array of tools will permit quite a large range of carving to be tackled. Many professionals do the bulk of their work with very few tools, but they have gradually built up their kits with tools to suit their needs. No one is ever likely to need all of the carving tools available, but the variety is there to permit a choice, suiting individual preferences and needs.

The tools are broadly divided into gouges, chisels and V tools, with a few special tools unlikely to be needed by the beginner. All tools are graded by width, in sizes from $\frac{1}{16}$ in. to $\frac{5}{8}$ in. The carvers most important tools are his gouges.

Gouges are made in a range of curves for each width. These go from almost flat to a very deep U-section. The degree of curvature is identified by a number. All widths do not have the same radius curve, but they have the same relative curve, e.g. a No. 9 straight gouge has an approximately semi-circular cross-section, whatever its width (Fig. 1A). Gouges with the lower numbers have flatter curves and those with higher numbers have deeper curves.

The common gouges are straight (Fig. 1B), but they may also be curved (Fig. 1C), spoon bit or front bent (Fig. 1D), back bent (Fig. 1E), spade or fish tail (Fig. 1F). While the beginner should know of these variations, he only needs a few straight gouges in his first kit. The varying shapes have different numbers from the straight tools. The numbers given (Fig. 1A) refer only to straight tools. Very small gouges may also be called "fluters" or "veiners".

Chisels are less frequently needed. They are normally ground on both sides like a turning tool (Fig. 1G). The end may be square or skew, as shown. Chisels are also made in the various bent shapes described for gouges. A spoon-bit skew chisel may be right or left cornered, depending on which side is foremost.

V tools, or parting tools, are a form of two-sided chisel. They are available with two different angles between the sides. Approximately, the wider angle made is 90°, the narrower 60°. The latter (No. 39) suits most jobs (Fig. 1H). V tools are normally straight (Fig. 1I), but they are also obtainable curved or spoon-bit, in the same way as gouges.

The amateur intending to tackle fairly light surface decoration will find that he can manage with half-a-dozen gouges, a V tool and a couple of chisels. A pen knife or wood-working marking knife will be useful.

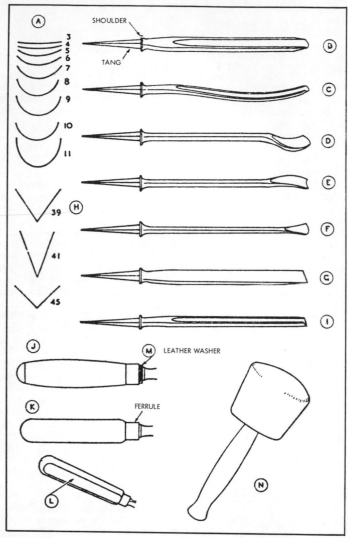

FIG. 1

Other tools can be added as the need for them is felt. A suitable first six gouges would be straight ones as follows: $\frac{1}{2}$ in. No. 5, $\frac{3}{8}$ in. No. 5, $\frac{1}{4}$ in. No. 6, $\frac{3}{8}$ in. No. 6, $\frac{1}{4}$ in. No. 7, $\frac{1}{2}$ in. No. 8. The V Tool should be $\frac{1}{4}$ in. No. 39. The chisels could be $\frac{1}{2}$ in. No. 1 Square and $\frac{1}{4}$ in. No. 2 Skew. Later tools could include a $\frac{1}{16}$ in. Veiner No. 47, a $\frac{1}{4}$ in. Bent Gouge No. 14, and a $\frac{1}{8}$ in. Spoon-bit Chisel No. 21 (See list of sets of tools at the end of this book). Additional gouges are always a good investment.

If handles have to be bought separately, choose stout ones for the tools which will be hit and slender ones for the more delicate tools intended only for hand work. The common handle shapes are slightly barrel-form (Fig. 1J) or parallel (Fig. 1K). Some workers prefer to have a flat planed on the underside of a handle (Fig. 1L). This allows the tool to approach the work at a flatter angle, which is an advantage in some awkward situations, and also prevents the tool rolling off the bench. There is something psychological about the quality of a handle—a nicely polished handle makes for better carving than a dirty ragged one, even when the blades are the same.

Fitting handles is a straightforward job. The important thing is a straight tight fit. A new handle may have a centre marked at the end. Drill into this with a twist drill about the same size as the small end of the tang. Go the full depth of the tang, and have an assistant watching to see that the hole is in line with the handle, by checking the angle you hold the brace. Enlarge the hole in steps, so that the tang of the tool can be pushed in rather more than half way by hand. It should be a slightly easier fit in box wood than in beech or ash, in that order. Support the tool in the vice, so that the shoulder rests on the top of the jaws, and tap the handle on. Examine it for straightness before driving fully home. When partly in, it may be possible to pull it straight or to pack the hole into line with a shaving.

Using a carving tool which has its handle out of line with the blade can be disconcerting and may result in bad work. Some workers do not drive the handle fully home to the shoulder of the tool when first fitting it—about $\frac{1}{8}$ in. of the tang is left exposed to allow for taking up any slackness which may develop later. Tools which are frequently used with a mallet may have a leather washer slipped over the tang before it is driven into the handle. This may be an ordinary tap washer. It becomes squeezed between the shoulder and the end of the handle (Fig. 1M), cushioning some of the effect of the blows on the tool.

There are two multi-purpose tools which can be very useful in taking the place of some of the standard tools in light carving. These are the "Multicraft" and "Trix-Exacto" tools. Both consist of handles fitted with chucks, into which a variety of chisels, knives, gouges etc., can be locked. The blades are cheap and supplied already sharpened, so that duplicate tools can be kept and changed over—sharpening being postponed until several need attention. Sharpening equipment is dealt with later in this chapter.

Much carving is done by hand pressure only, but for heavy cuts a mallet is needed. An ordinary carpenter's mallet can be used, but the carver favours a special one with a round head (Fig. 1N) weighing about two pounds. Beech is the usual wood for mallets.

Various holding devices will be needed. These are described in Chapter 2. Rasps, files and punches are occasionally needed. Of course, carving is usually part of some structure, for which the general wood-working tools will be required.

Secondhand carving tools are often available. Common sense will be the best guide in assessing their value to the particular carver, but there are a few points to watch. Uncommon sizes and shapes are not much use, unless the tools are cheap and the carver already has the commoner basic tools and is seeking to extend his kit. The condition of handles is not important, as these are easily replaced. There is some advantage in having a variety of handles, as that helps in the identification of tools on the bench. Secondhand tools may have been neglected for some time. If they are pitted with rust they may be useless, unless the pitting is in a position that will be ground away during sharpening. Tools which have been broken and resharpened may still be quite useful, but they should be cheaper than longer tools. Tools which have the characteristic coarse sharp marks from having been ground on an engineer's high-speed grinding wheel should be accepted warily, as they may have been overheated and the resulting colours cleaned off to destroy the evidence of this softening.

SHARPENING

The maintenance of the finest possible cutting edge on his tools is probably more important to a wood carver than to any other craftsman in wood. It is therefore essential to master the not-too-difficult processes of tool sharpening and to carefully apply them whenever necessary. The work produced by a dull tool does not have the freshness and clean appearance that a keen edge produces, and it will always be obvious to another woodworker even if not to every layman.

A good quality tool, made from the correct grade of steel, accurately hardened and tempered, will keep its edge longer than an inferior tool. Fortunately, there is not a mass-market for carving tools, as there is for some types of general tools, so that the manufacturers of equipment for the carver are mostly specialist firms offering good-quality products. It is, however, good policy to always buy carving tools from a shop specializing in tools and to buy the best that one can afford.

Tool sharpening is divided into two main parts—grinding, which produces the bevel by the removal of the bulk of the metal; and sharpening proper, which is the production of the keen cutting edge. Grinding is only needed at comparatively long intervals, and it is possible to have this done professionally, but the keen worker usually wishes to have complete control over the treatment of his tools, as the bevel ground by someone else may not be exactly as required.

Grinding of woodworking tools is best done on a sandstone wheel. This need not be large—say twelve inches diameter and two inches wide—mounted in a trough for fixing to a bench. If access to a large workshop type grindstone is possible that is, of course, also suitable. The stone should be turned slowly away from the tool. Hold the tool with both hands, one on the handle maintaining the angle and the other over the blade applying the pressure. To avoid overheating and to prevent the stone clogging, it must be kept lubricated with water. This can be from a dripping can above the stone, or from water in the trough. In any case the trough should be emptied after use to avoid softening of the stone.

The angle and length of the bevel depends on the experience and preference of the carver. A long thin bevel takes a fine edge, but it will be weak and soon blunted. At the other extreme a tool sharpened with a very obtuse angle, will be robust but not so keen. Something between the two is usually required, with a tendency towards long bevels for work mainly on soft woods and a tendency towards short bevels for the harder woods. A grinding angle of about 20° is a good average. The length of the bevel is then about $\frac{3}{8}$ in.

To avoid uneven wear on the stone the tool should be moved from side to side across the curved surface. Tools with flat edges should be held steady, but gouges should be rolled at the same time as they are moved across the grindstone to keep an even bevel (Fig. 2A). After the correct bevel has been obtained, the back of the bevel should be rounded to blend into the line of the tool, so that there is no sudden change of angle.

Many amateur woodworkers now use a small engineer's type of high-speed grinding wheel, either power or hand driven. It is possible to grind carving tools on this, but very great care is needed to avoid overheating. The stone turns towards the tool at a high speed, and the thin steel edge can quickly overheat to the point where the temper is drawn, leaving the tool soft. If colours appear near the edge it is a sign that this has happened, and nothing can be done about it, except grind past the limit of the colours. If one of these grinding wheels has to be used, the tools must be very frequently removed from the wheel and dipped in water.

After grinding, the tools are sharpened on an oilstone. Two grades are needed—one fairly coarse, such as "Carborundum" or "India", and another finer one. Old craftsmen have preferences for special oils, but the lightest machine oil or paraffin will be found suitable. If a stone becomes clogged with dirt or thick oil, it can be freed by soaking in paraffin. Besides flat stones about eight inches long, a few slips (Fig. 2B) are needed for the inside surfaces of shaped tools. A slip with its edges shaped to two different curves will deal with the first few gouges

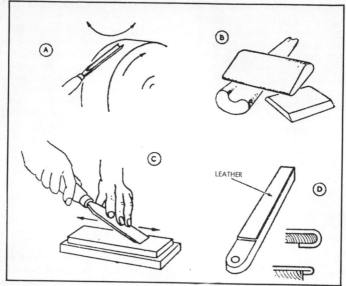

FIG. 2

of a beginner's kit. One with a sharp edge is needed for the inside of the V tool.

A straight-edge tool is held on the oilstone in the same way as on the grindstone, and rubbed steadily backwards and forwards (Fig. 2C) over the surface of the oilstone. The angle should be slightly higher than when grinding, so that the cutting edge receives the pressure and the back of the bevel is just clear of the surface. At first there will be a tendency to dip the hands at the far end of the stroke, but this must be resisted and the bevel maintained constant. The chisel edge may be sharpened with a bevel one side only, both sides equally, or mainly one side, as preferred.

When the edge appears sharp, check this by rubbing the finger over the other surface towards the edge. If the edge is sharp, a roughness will be felt. This is the tiny particle of steel rubbed off the edge, but still just clinging to it. This burr, or "wire edge", must be rubbed off by a few strokes of the other side flat against the stone.

After treatment on the coarse stone, the process is repeated on the fine stone. Curved tools are treated in the same way, except that when dealing with an outside curve on a flat stone the gouge should be rolled. It may be held in line with the stone and rolled from side to side while being pushed backwards and forwards, although some workers prefer to hold the gouge at an angle to the stone, when viewed from above, so that it is rubbed with a rolling action along the stone. Gouges and V tools should be sharpened on the two grades of stone in the same way as described for chisels, but the burr must be removed by rubbing on the inside with suitable slips.

Sharpening on a stone is the final treatment in preparing ordinary woodworking tools, but carving tools are usually brought to an even finer finish by stropping. The strop is a piece of leather glued to a strip of wood. Its surface is treated with a fine abrasive. Pumice powder or the finest emery powder, mixed with vaseline, can be worked into the leather. Crocus powder produces an even finer finish. To strop a tool, both sides are drawn several times over the leather. A curved edge to the strop (Fig. 2D) will go inside most gouges.

Once a tool has been brought to a fine edge it can be maintained for some time by merely repeating the last stages. In use, slight dullness will soon be sensed, and for the first few times this can usually be righted by a few rubs on the strop. Later, treatment on the fine oilstone followed by stropping, will be needed. After a long interval, it will be necessary to go back to the coarse oilstone stage, and at very long intervals re-grinding will be necessary.

There are a few special points in the sharpening of carving tools, which should be noted, particularly by those already experienced in dealing with general woodworking tools:

1. Chisels, whether square or skew, should have straight cutting edges. They may have bevels both sides. The sharpening bevel usually blends into the grinding bevel, which in turn blends into the back of the tool, so that there are no distinct changes of angle as in firmer chisels.

2. Gouges should be sharpened so that they are square across the end, except perhaps for a very small rounding of the corners. A gouge pressed straight down on to a piece of wood should leave its shape evenly pressed into the surface. Similarly, the two sides of a V tool should be sharpened equally and with their edges level.

3. Some carvers rub away the insides of gouges so that a second bevel is formed there. This slightly increases the size of the curve of the end and may minimize digging in when the gouge is used with the convex side outside, but for normal work it does not make much difference. If the inside is to be bevelled, it involves considerable rubbing with slips, as the inside cannot be ground.

4. Fluters and the deeper gouges (Nos. 10 and 11) are U-shaped, instead of parts of regular curves in cross-section. The bottom has a quick curve, but the sides are almost straight. When grinding or sharpening, the rolling of the edge to keep the wear even should be confined to a half of the curve at a time, or the bottom curve may be dealt with first, followed by the sides separately.

5. Stropping the inside of the smallest gouges is difficult. One way

is to draw the gouge along the edge of the leather several times so that one point rests over the edge and the leather is compressed to fit inside the tool.

6. A V tool is sharpened on the inside with a knife-edged slip, but the most difficult part is at the point where the two sides meet. This needs to be sharp and without burr, otherwise it will not cut cleanly, but will tear the wood. If the point of the V becomes spiky (the point projecting forward of the cutting edges), this can be reduced by rounding the junction between the two bevels on the outside, and working carefully on the inside with a slip.

Obviously tools to which so much care is given in sharpening must have their edges protected during storage. Throwing together in a drawer will soon damage edges. A baize, or canvas, roll, with a pocket for each tool can be used, or they can be fitted into racks inside a cupboard. It is worth while arranging for the edges to be visible, so that they can easily be selected for use. When stored for some time the steel parts should be coated with oil or one of the rust inhibiting fluids.

WOODS FOR CARVING

Any wood may be carved, with varying results, but wood is a natural product and characteristics vary between the woods of different trees and even between different members of the same tree family. Wood for carving should usually be of uniform, even grain, free from large knots or violent contrasts in the appearance of the grain. Sometimes a pronounced grain marking may be used by a clever craftsman to enhance the appearance of a piece of work, but normally an inconspicuous grain is preferred.

There are other characteristics to consider. Ease of working is important, but the very easy working woods have no great strength or durability, so that in most cases they are only suitable for practise work. The type of carving should be considered. Some woods are more suitable for fine delicate work, while others lend themselves better to broad robust treatment. Some woods will not last long if exposed to the elements, while others contain natural oils which protect them against the weather.

All wood used for carving should be properly seasoned. Most woods season best if felled in the autumn. Seasoning (the drying out of a proportion of the moisture in the wood) takes many years if done naturally, but modern methods reduce this time to a matter of weeks. Artificially seasoned wood is quite satisfactory. Unseasoned wood will crack and warp. Even seasoned wood may crack or warp if subjected to violent changes of temperature or humidity—some woods more than others.

Some woods may develop "shakes" (cracks) during working, as new surfaces are uncovered. The internal stresses in the wood, causing these cracks, are usually more pronounced in large pieces than small. It is sometimes possible to reduce the effective bulk of a carved piece. A solid model can have a large hole drilled up some way from the base. A plaque can have the back hollowed. Both methods relieve strain and minimize the risk of warping and cracking.

If cracks develop while working, they may close up again as the job progresses. It is unwise to try to fill them with wood, as this may cause them to spread. Beeswax can be used while the work progresses. This protects the edges from splintering during cutting, and as it never sets hard it can squeeze out if the crack closes. If a crack appears to be permanent, it can be filled with plastic wood. Natural cracks should not often prove troublesome, but if they do appear they are not likely to detract from the effect of the finished job.

Since the war hundreds of new timbers have come into this country, mostly from the Empire. These are known loosely as "Empire hardwoods". Most come in small quantities and may not be seen again, so that it is difficult to classify them. Others seem to have considerable possibilities for the carver. There are certain traditional woods, which have been found by experience to be suitable for carving, and the beginner is best advised to confine his work to them at first, then if he is offered a strange wood he may be able to assess its qualities from its appearance or by testing a piece and comparing it with a better-known wood.

Following are the names of some of the more usual traditional woods, with a few notes on their characteristics:

Oak. Most carving in this country has been done in oak. It is durable, strong and it has attractive colour and grain. It is most suitable for bold treatment. All oaks are rather tough to carve—English oak being particularly so. Austrian oak has straighter grain. American is best avoided.

Walnut. There are several walnuts. Most have even, close grain and are suitable for carving. Appearance is good, and the wood is not so tough as oak to carve.

Satin walnut. This is not a true walnut. It has a pale brown colour with no great contrast in the grain. It is an easy wood to work and suitable for early exercises. It has a tendency to warp long after it has been worked.

Pine. This is a soft wood. It is light in colour and one of the easiest woods to cut. It is suitable for practice work, but dull tools will be found to crush and tear it.

Mahogany. The name covers a large family of trees. Most are suitable for carving, with qualities similar to walnut. African mahogany is not generally as suitable as that from Honduras.

Sycamore, lime and pear. All three are light-coloured woods with close grain, suitable for delicate work.

Birch. This is medium hard and pleasant to work, but it is not very durable.

Teak. Its working qualities are similar to oak, although it quickly blunts tools. It is the best wood for outdoor work.

Jarrah. This is a red Australian wood, suitable for outdoor work. It carves evenly.

Ebony and lignum vitae. These are extremely hard woods, the latter being the heaviest known wood. They are carved by the experts, but are unsuitable for those less experienced.

CHAPTER II

TOOL HANDLING

MAKING the tools carry out your wishes is largely a matter of experience gained by practice. Once the technique is mastered, one can reach a stage where the selection and handling of the tools calls for so little thought that most of the attention can be given to the artistic side of the work. Care in using the tools in the right way and for their correct job is important at the start, so as to lay the right foundations. An intelligent appreciation of the behaviour of the wood under the tools is essential. Learn by your mistakes—if anything goes wrong, think out the cause of the trouble.

Wood is a fibrous material, with the fibres laid more or less lengthwise. If all of these fibres are considered to be loose, the effect of the tool can be understood. There is usually one direction in which the tools cut in the cleanest way. Cutting the opposite way produces a rough surface. If the tool is made to cut diagonally along the fibres they will part smoothly (Fig. 3A). If it is entered the opposite way, they will catch in the tool edge and tear up (Fig. 3B). The direction of the grain can usually be observed and its reaction to a cut forecast, but grain is often far from straight and anything doubtful should be tackled warily to avoid splitting. A gouge is a safer tool than a chisel, particularly if it is entered across the grain, not necessarily at right angles. Its curved edges cut the fibres before the lower part of the blade has a chance of getting under them and levering them up, if the grain happens to be awkward.

Carving tools may be used with hand pressure, or by hitting with a mallet. In the preliminary "bosting-in"—i.e. knocking into shape, by cutting away the bulk of the unwanted wood—most of the work is done with a large gouge and a mallet. The tool is held in the left hand, with the fingers around the handle and the thumb along it at the end away from the blade (Fig. 3C). The stance should be easy—it is a mistake to hold yourself rigid when carving. The weight of blows will depend on the material, but normally the mallet should only be lifted a few inches from the tool handle. It is very useful to be able to use carving tools in either hand, so practise changing over.

Hand work is used for the more delicate finishing operations, or for heavier cuts in soft wood. Both hands should always be on the tool. One hand provides the pressure, while the other restrains and guides the tool. Normally the right hand is over the end of the handle, grasping it securely. The left hand is over the blade—maybe not much more than the finger tips for very light cuts, but more usually the fingers are around the blade and the thumb pointing up the handle (Fig. 3D). In this way

17

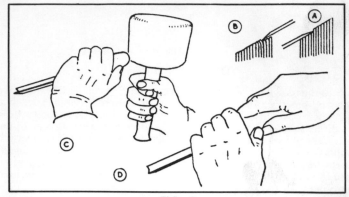

FIG. 3

the right hand presses forward, but the left hand has the "feel" of the cut, steering the edge where it is needed, steadying it on its course, and ever-ready to restrain it if the grain gives too readily or the cut is completed.

While the worker should have an easy stance and avoid rigidity in himself, the reverse is the rule for the article being carved. Good work can only be done when cuts can be made confidently without worrying about the possibility of the work moving. It is not always easy to hold a complex job, and holding devices will have to improvised. Vices will hold many jobs, but their jaws should be covered with soft wood or cloth to prevent damage. Some work may be screwed to scrap wood which can be held between the vice jaws. A vice is not always the best means of holding a large piece of wood, as the weight overhanging the bench is badly placed for stability.

Much early work will be done on flat pieces of wood. These can be held on the top of the bench in a number of ways. Ordinary G cramps may be suitable, but their projection above the work may be a nuisance and necessitate moving them around. The lighter type made from flat strip have less projection, but they are only strong enough for light work. A cabinetmaker's holdfast (Fig. 4A) may be fixed through a hole in a stout bench top where the edge does not permit cramps, but like them it may be in the way of some tool operations.

One way of holding flat work, without projections above the surface level is to nail or screw blocks to the bench around the wood. Three of these may touch the edges, but the fourth is far enough away to admit a pair of folding wedges, which are driven in from opposite sides to lock the work (Fig. 4B). A cam with a loose bar is an alternative locking

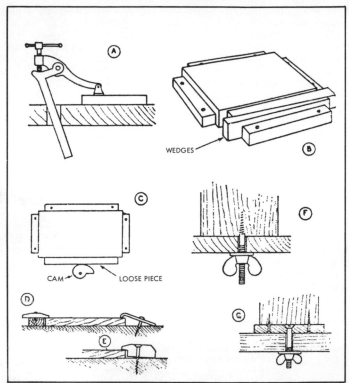

WEDGES

CAM → LOOSE PIECE

FIG. 4

device (Fig. 4C). However a flat job is held, it will be necessary to lift it and clean out shavings and dust occasionally, and it is convenient to be able to turn it round, so the mounting should not be too securely fixed to the bench. Small turnbuttons on blocks of the same thick.ness as the board are another method (Fig. 4D). Wood or metal dogs can be used (Fig. 4E).

Sometimes the work may be arranged so that part of the waste wood is not cut away until after the carving is completed. Screws or cramps can then hold the waste wood. Holding devices which involve screwing to, or otherwise making holes in the bench, should be used sparingly, otherwise the bench top will become damaged and unsuitable for other work.

If the work has an irregular outline, a baseboard projecting a little all round can be temporarily screwed to the underside, then this screwed or cramped to the bench. Mounting on a temporary baseboard is a useful method for many examples of carving. As an alternative to screwing, paper can be glued to the back and the base-board glued to this. The joint will hold during carving, but the parts are easily separated with a knife or chisel when the work is finished.

Carvers' bench screws (Fig. 4F) are suitable for holding thick work, particularly when carving figures in the solid, as they permit the job to be turned round. The tapered screw is driven into a hole drilled in the bottom of the work, or the baseboard to which it is fixed. The long threaded portion then passes through a hole in the bench and is locked by a large wing nut and washer. A similar idea may be improvised with an ordinary bolt, which is passed through a baseboard before it is fixed to the work (Fig. 4G).

It is unwise to attempt a design for actual use, until some experience has been gained in tool handling. At first odd pieces of wood should be cut in various ways so that what a tool cannot do, as well as what it can do, is discovered. Make cuts by hand and with a mallet, across and in line with the grain. Practise controlling the depth of the cut, by raising or lowering the angle of approach of the tool. Learn to take sweeping cuts, so as to follow a curve, while keeping the depth even. Do this with the gouges and the V tool. Outline a shape with the V tool or deep gouge, and remove the waste with a gouge. Make cuts diagonally and vertically to the surface of the wood.

Much cutting with gouges and chisels will have to be straightforward pushing or hitting, but where the circumstances allow, the tool may be handled with a slicing action. It will then cut cleaner, with less tendency to tear out the grain. The difference in action is comparable to cutting a piece of string with a knife—if the knife is simply pushed into the string it may eventually cut if sufficient force is applied, but if it is sliced across the string much less effort will be required. A slicing action is usually possible with the flatter gouges working on a broad surface or background. Practise making slicing cuts, both in hollowing and external rounding. Usually the wrist of the restraining hand should rest against the work or the bench.

It is very convenient to be able to use tools in either hand. Both hands are usually on the tool in any case, but the right-handed man will always want to hold the handle in his right hand while the left restrains. No carver is likely to become ambidextrous to the point where he does not favour one grip more than another, but the ability to change hands is so valuable as to be worth practising from the start.

Gouge cuts look best when completed with one stroke. With changing curves this may not be possible, and in any case the beginner tends to take small bites at the wood. Even when most of a hollow is dug out timidly in this way, a final cut in one sweep should be taken to finish it off.

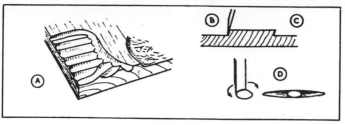

FIG. 5

A "quick" gouge (i.e. one with a sharp curvature in its section) can cut more deeply than a flatter gouge. Gouges are sometimes described as "flat". This is a relative term and does not mean that the gouge is absolutely flat (if it was it would be a chisel). It is a name given to the gouges with the slightest curvature (Nos. 3 and 4). A carver usually favours a flat gouge for work where the joiner or cabinetmaker would use a chisel. In sinking a ground the general shape may be outlined with a quick gouge, which is then used to remove the bulk if the waste (Fig. 5A). This is followed by a flat gouge to produce the final surface of the background by cutting diagonally across the grain. Although the final background will be of uniform depth, its surface will be covered with the flat gouge marks, and nothing is done to remove them. This is a characteristic carver's finish and it should not be further levelled by work with a router, as a cabinetmaker may feel tempted to do. Recessing in this way occurs in much carving, and the process should be practised.

When bosting-in, to remove waste, with a mallet and a large gouge, cuts are usually made diagonally across the grain. Providing the points of the cutting edge are kept above the surface of the wood, quite heavy cuts can be taken with little fear of splitting the wood. Practise on scrap wood, to discover the most efficient way of removing waste, before bosting-in an actual job.

Designs are usually "cut in" so that their edges slope outwards to a background (Fig. 5B). This is done mainly for strength. The reverse is called "undercutting" (Fig. 5C), and is employed when the design is to appear to stand out prominently above the lower part. Undercutting makes the depth appear more by increasing the shadow. Cutting in should be done with tools which approximate to the outline. To avoid breaking out of the grain, cuts should go from "with the grain" to "across the grain", not vice versa.

Cutting in small circles for the centres of flowers or beads on a moulding, can be done by pressing the end of a gouge straight down and rotating it. Each gouge will cut a circle of one size (Fig. 5D), and the depth can be increased by further rotating and pressing the gouge. With his limited equipment the beginner should keep a record of the outlines of his tools, and the circles they will cut, so that designs can be adapted to suit the tools available. Pressing the tools into cardboard or plywood is one way of making the record. Where tools do not conform exactly to a shape, the cutting in can be corrected by slicing with a skew chisel or knife.

Try out various woods. Although the technique may be the same in principle, a change from soft to hard wood can be deceptive and may lead to damaged work if unprepared. Get to know all of your tools. Learn how much pressure to apply on various woods. Learn, also, how to identify the first signs of dullness; how the cut loses its cleanness and the tool is due for stropping or sharpening.

CHAPTER III

SIMPLE DECORATION

MANY readers of this book will already be woodworkers, looking to carving as something on which to further practise their skill, and as a means of embellishing their constructional work. The items in this chapter are not carving in its most ambitious sense, but are intended to supply ideas for applying carving methods to the simple decoration of ordinary woodworking projects. Most of the work can be done with knives and ordinary woodworking chisels and gouges if proper carving tools are not available.

The old-time wheelwright, doing most of his work with a draw-knife, sought relief from the heavy constructional work by using the same tool to nick patterns in the edges of parts of a wagon. This form of decoration is now generally called "wagon bevelling", and it can be developed to give a pleasing effect on such things as stool and table legs. Apart from any decorative value in itself, it has the effect of lightening the appearance of a necessarily stout part of the structure without weakening it.

The simplest wagon bevelling has a long parallel chamferred edge stopping in a triangular cut (Fig. 6A). Pencil guide lines are drawn, then the ends cut and the chamfer carefully pared with a chisel. The next step in this form of decoration is to replace the simple triangle with curved cuts (Fig. 6B). Instead of the long parallel part the cuts may be a series of curves and notches (Fig. 6C). The best effect is obtained by avoiding very heavy cuts—wagon bevelling is most effective when comparatively small.

Much of the work can be done freehand, with guide lines pencilled on each surface, governing the width, and other marks to show the length of each pattern. Most cuts are made with the chisel, used in line with the work. If an ordinary chisel is used, its bevel should be downwards when scooping out curved chamfers, and its flat side down for straight cuts. A variation is to use a gouge in line with the edge, following the same pattern, but leaving a chamfer which is hollow in cross-section. Of course, if a draw-knife or a spokeshave are available the work may be done with them in the traditional way. Files and rasps are out of place in this work. They leave evidence of inferior workmanship for all to see.

The range of wagon bevelling designs is governed only by the carver's imagination. When working out patterns, sharp points should be avoided as they may crumble. Short flats are better (Fig. 6D). Besides legs, this treatment can also be effectively applied to book ends, rails, shelves and table tops. Most of the original wheelwright's work was in ash, oak, elm and other native British hardwoods, so that articles made

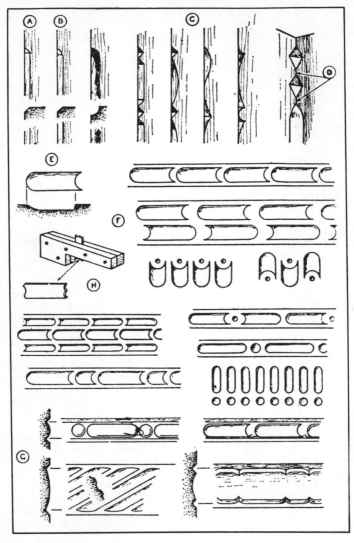

FIG. 6

from these woods are particularly appropriate for this sort of decoration, but it can be used with restraint on many other woods.

Experiments with gouges will show that they lend themselves to simple decorative cuts, suggested by their shapes. Gouge work can produce attractive borders and edges simply by the repetition of a groove worked by one gouge. The basic cutting consists of a near vertical cut followed by a scoop towards it with the same gouge (Fig. 6E). Points to watch are: a vertical cut is not as strong or attractive as a slightly sloping one (undercutting by sloping the other way is to be avoided), and a groove which goes to its full depth quickly and remains parallel is more effective than one with a tapering depth.

In soft wood the upright cuts may be made by hand pressure, but in hard wood a mallet may be needed. A depth of $\frac{1}{8}$ in. is usually sufficient. In scooping out the waste, the full depth should be reached in a few cuts. This gives a cleaner result as the gouge has to cut into the bottom of the upright cut at the end of the horizontal stroke, and if many fine cuts are taken they will penetrate this end and disfigure or weaken it.

Many variations of gouge designs are possible, and a few examples are shown (Fig. 6F). Marking out can be confined to parallel guide lines and marks where the upright cuts are to come. It is best to systematically cut all the near-vertical edges first—depth is then more likely to be even, and there is less risk of the crumbling which may occur when a vertical cut is made near the start of a horizontal one. Dots are made by rotating a small gouge until the waste wood falls out.

Gouge decoration is particularly appropriate to edges of shelves and other horizontal parts, where the light shining from above, catches the cuts and shows them to advantage. It can also be used to form a border on an end member, such as a book-end. Where moulding planes, or other means of forming a bead, are available the carving may be done on a curved surface to produce another attractive effect (Fig. 6G). Balls and ovals can be built into many patterns on beads. This type of decoration will relieve the severity of modern designs if worked along the lower edges of rails under table tops and shelves.

'An alternative to a moulding plane for working beads and other shapes is called a "scratch stock" (Fig. 6H). This is a form of scraper which works well on hardwoods. The blade is a piece of tool steel (stout clock spring will do) with its end ground to the required shape. Single and double beads are common forms. Grinding can be done on the corner of a grindstone, and is done straight across the thickness of the end, with no attempt to sharpen in the ordinary way. It is the burr on the squared edge which does the cutting. The blade can be clamped between the split sides of a marking gauge or between two shaped pieces of wood. It is used with a rubbing action, the top of the blade sloping towards the direction of the cut, in the same way as a marking gauge. One advantage of the scratch stock over the moulding plane is that beads can be stopped before reaching the edge, while a moulding plane

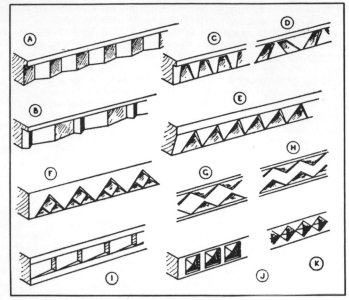

FIG. 7

will only cut if taken right through from edge to edge.

Chisels and knives can also be used to make edge decorations. The upright cuts should again be slightly off of vertical, for strength and appearance, and they should be made first. The waste is removed by paring towards the upright cuts. A depth of ⅛ in. is usually enough. Chisel cuts are most effective on horizontal members, such as edges of table tops, shelves or cabinet tops. In most cases the effect is improved if the cuts are made in a shallow rebate, planed so as to leave a narrow overhang at the top. More detailed marking out is advisable, as accuracy is more necessary in straight line decoration than with curves. Innumerable variations will suggest themselves. Simple geometrical forms are most effective.

In the first example (Fig. 7A) the edge is decorated with angular corrugations. Pencil lines mark the ridges and hollows, then the hollows are cut straight in to full depth with a knife or chisel and the waste pared away towards this cut. Variety can be obtained by varying the size of the corrugations (Fig. 7B) or making their slopes uneven.

An effective way of catching the light is to cut grooves into the edge at intervals. These taper in depth and may have parallel or tapered sides

(Fig. 7C). They may be at right angles to the edge of sloping one or both ways (Fig. 7D). After marking out, the cuts across the grain are made first, followed by the cut marking the deeper end of the hollow, then the waste is pared out. A tapered groove is easier to clean out than a parallel one, while sloping grooves will need a knife in the acute corners.

Dog tooth decoration will be found in many old churches. It was a favourite method of the old-time stone workers. The work may be done on a flat edge, under a rebate, or on a slight chamfer, as shown (Fig. 7E). If the shapes are set out so that the angle at the point of the cut is slightly more than a right-angle an ordinary chisel can be used, but if it is less, a skew chisel will be needed to remove the waste. In this and most repetition decoration it is best to treat the strip as a whole, doing the same cut to each pattern in turn. This will ensure a more uniform result than if each pattern is completed individually.

After cutting a row of single dog-tooth triangles, the recesses can be treated in the same way again (Fig. 7F). Do not make the first cuts too deep for this pattern. Dog-toothing worked from both sides will produce diamonds (Fig. 7G) or a zig-zag (Fig. 7H), which can also be found in old churches. When cutting the diamonds it is safer to leave a small flat between them. This is stronger and usually easier to cut.

A variation of the first pattern can be worked between parallel sides (Fig. 7I). This can be used on vertical edges, with the long slopes upwards, then the narrow slopes make good shadows and do not catch the dust. A simple way of working this pattern is to cut in the sides first with a cutting gauge to the full depth of the grooves. The short slopes are then cut and the waste pared towards them.

Another pattern, giving good practice in chisel control is cutting square buttons, which may be upright (Fig. 7J) or diamond fashion (Fig. 7K). Squares are drawn to suit the width of the chisel, which is then pressed vertically in all round. Each button is then pared with the same chisel from the centre outwards, cutting the faces with the grain first. Similar type buttons may have five or six sides. They can be placed individually or in a series.

There may be a temptation in gouge and chisel work to touch up inaccuracies or rough parts with glasspaper or a file, but this should be avoided, as any rounding of corners will spoil the characteristic clean-cut appearance that distinguishes it from the inferior machine-made decorations.

CHIP CARVING

Chip carving is probably the oldest form of carving. It is not now as popular as in the past, but the amateur craftsman is not ruled by fashion and is free to use what methods he chooses. Chip carving can be used to decorate many articles, and it has the advantage of not needing many tools. It looks best on small articles. All-over chip carving on fairly large items of furniture, as once practised, does not look right to modern eyes. A single chip carved pattern as a centre piece or a simple pattern worked as a border will look well on such things as book ends, pot stands, paper knives, box tops, or drawer fronts.

The design is arranged so that nearly all of the cuts are triangular. The sides of the triangle may be curved, even to the extent of two curves combining to form one sweep, but apart from this the basic cuts can be considered to be three-sided. There are no flat-bottomed recesses. Nearly all of the work is done with a knife, although chisels and gouges can be used effectively on some patterns. The knife may be of the pocket variety or a marking knife pattern, with the cutting edge skew across the end. In any case the edge should be fine and kept sharp.

Practise on scrap wood, cutting the typical recesses, or "pockets". Draw a triangular outline, with lines in to meet at the centre (Fig. 8A). Cut along these centre lines with a knife held vertically, the cut tapering from about ⅛ in. deep at the centre to nothing at the corners (Fig. 8B). Next, remove the waste, tapering each side down to the centre, by paring with a knife or chisel in a series of slices, removing chips of wood, from which the process gets its name (Fig. 8C), until the three bevels meet at the centre (Fig. 8D).

Where a pocket has curved sides, the centre cuts must also curve upwards from the centre to the corners. This is best done by cutting from each end in turn, increasing the pressure towards the centre (Fig. 8E). The direction of the grain must be considered when slicing out waste, but where this permits, the curved sides of the pocket should be sliced from opposite ends. Several cuts are needed; and the last cut with a sharp blade should leave a clean accurate surface as it takes off the last shaving. The knife can be used in one hand, while the other holds and turns the wood to the best position, but care should be taken to never cut towards the other hand. It is probably wiser to use the knife two-handed, as described for the carving tools, with one hand pressing and the other guiding and restraining.

Designs for chip carving are usually geometric. They should be marked out completely, including the centre cuts, using pencil, rule, square and compass—either directly on the wood or on paper for tracing through.

Variations on a star form, with radiating points like a mariner's compass, are the basis of many chip carving designs (Fig. 8F). Altering the points to curves produces a conventionalized floral pattern (Fig. 8G). Corners can be treated by portions of these designs (Fig. 8H). Triangles can be built up into many border designs (Fig. 8I). Repetition of a comparatively simple pattern is usually more effective than a striving after complication. All-over patterns can be used for small panels or centre pieces. Again simplicity is best (Fig. 8J). From these basic patterns and their variations decorations can be built up to suit particular jobs.

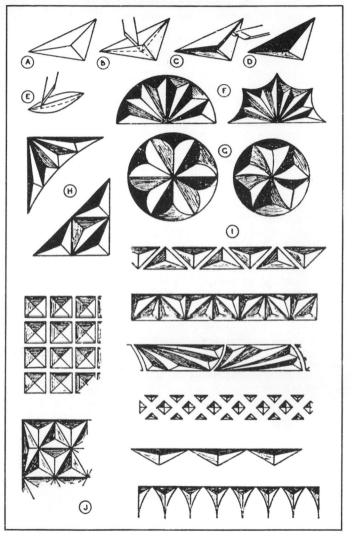

FIG. 8

Wood with an even grain is best for chip carving. A pronounced grain, with varying degrees of hardness, may deflect the blade of the knife, even more than it would a stouter gouge or chisel. Much oak is too harsh for chip carving, although it looks attractive if success is achieved. Pine or a mild variety of mahogany are easier to chip carve.

WHITTLING

In soft wood with a mild grain much carving can be done with a sharp knife as the only tool. This is commonly termed whittling and serves as an introduction to carving for many people—success at carving with a knife has produced the urge to progress further. Whittling as an activity in its own right is more popular in the U.S.A., possibly because suitable wood is more common and the work is very similar to the carving done by Red Indians.

Whittling certainly teaches the worker the effect of tools on wood and helps him to instinctively feel the behaviour of grain—he will almost certainly spoil much wood due to unpredicted splits, or unsatisfactory tool control. The beginner tends to hold the wood in one hand and whittle with the other. It is much better to fasten the work down, by cramping, screwing or holding in a vice. It is usually better to have two hands on the knife—one pushing and the other controlling or restraining, as with proper carving tools. Apart from the gain in tool control, this is much safer.

Much whittling consists of taking a natural stick, the shape of which suggests the object being carved, or of working the design on a round pole. Much native carving, especially that intended for sale, is whittled in this way. Walking-stick handles form an interesting outlet for whittling. Natural crooks and joints may suggest animal heads or other forms which can be shaped with a knife. The addition of a coping saw or "Abrafile" allows work to be done in the solid. Waste is sawn away and the object finished by whittling.

One example of native carving which mystifies the tourist, is a wooden chain, often finishing in a spoon or mascot. The wooden links are solid and without glued-up breaks. Making a series of wooden links is comparatively simple. This is also interesting as a method of cutting a piece of wood so that it is longer after it is cut.

A strip of wood is cut to a cross cross-section (Fig. 9A). The thickness of each arm is a little more than the thickness each link is to be. This shaping may be done with a rebate plane or fillister, or with a circular saw. If none of these methods is possible it can be whittled roughly to shape, but this will involve more cleaning up later.

The lengths and then the shapes of the links are marked out with an allowance for waste between them. The links one way come midway between those the other way (Fig. 9B). Holes are drilled through the waste wood to allow a fretsaw blade to pass through. One link at a time should be concentrated on—only sufficient work being done to

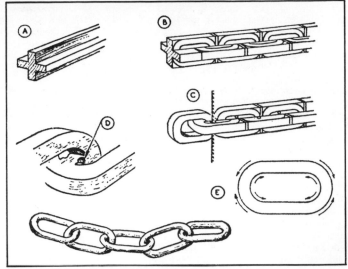

FIG. 9

following links to free the one being worked. The outside is sawn or whittled. The end of the next link is shaped to remove wood which might interfere with getting tools into the first link. Much of the inside wood is removed by fretsawing (Fig. 9C) from the first and second links. They are separated by drilling small holes diagonally between them (Fig. 9D), followed by carefully whittling with a fine-pointed knife. Clean off fibres still clinging as the parts separate.

The first link may be finally shaped at this stage, or it can be left until all of the links are freed. Shaping of the links to a round cross-section is done with a knife having a long tapered blade. Care is needed where there is short grain at the end of each link. On the inside the knife should cut from the end to the side, but on the outside it should cut from the side to the end (Fig. 9E).

CHAPTER IV

INCISED CARVING

Success in carving depends very largely on exact tool control, and it is as well to spend some time on comparatively simple jobs which provide practice in tool handling, without making too great demands on skill. Work can be selected which gives satisfying results, yet is within the range of a beginner's ability. This is far better than plunging into a difficult design which may only lead to disappointment. The gouge cuts and edge decorations, described in the last chapter, are in the intermediate class. Another type of work with possibilities for decorating actual articles, is incised carving.

Incised carving is basically the cutting in of a pattern, either with a knife or a V tool. This may be elaborated by colouring and punching backgrounds. One of the knives fitting the Multicraft or Trix-Exacto handles is convenient for this work. Another knife, not originally intended for carving, but which is very convenient and easy to control, is a linoleum knife. With one or both hands on it, the low angle of the handle makes it easy to follow lines (Fig. 10A).

Incising with a knife is a little more difficult than a V tool, but the result is neater. If a V tool is used, the acute-angled one (No. 41) is most suitable. With a knife, the object is to make two slightly sloping cuts so as to remove a small sliver of wood between them (Fig. 10B). Great depth is not so important as cleanness of cut, so the point of the knife should be kept in perfect condition. Straight lines may be cut with the knife against a rule. It is best to always work away from the junction of two lines, to minimize the risk or over-running.

Straight cuts can be made with one hand on the knife and the other on the rule or straight-edge. Curves are cut with both hands on the knife, as with other carving tools. While the pressure needed will cause some tensioning of the muscles, the hands and arms should be kept as loose and free as possible, to follow curves with a sweep, rather than with a jerking motion, which will produce minute zig-zags instead of a free-flowing curve.

Geometric patterns can be worked out on paper (Fig. 10C) and transferred to the wood with carbon paper. Borders are particularly appropriate. Formal flowers and foliage can be drawn (Fig. 10D). In all of these patterns very acute junctions between lines should be avoided as far as possible, in case the wood crumbles there.

Incising patterns or pictures and colouring the spaces is known as "intarsia" or "tarso" work. The effect is rather like veneering or marquetry, except that the colour is applied to the one piece of wood,

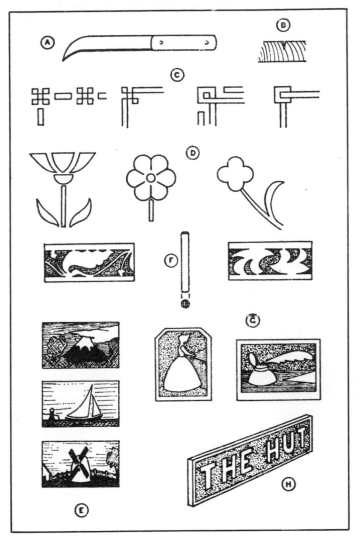

FIG. 10

instead of being built up from separate woods of different colours. For this work the design chosen should have bold outlines to the various parts (Fig. 10E). All of the lines are incised, and care taken to see that they are free from dust or shavings, so that each area is completely surrounded by a channel. This is important, as the channel prevents the colours running, and a part uncut or a channel blocked, may provide a path for the colour to pass over into the next area.

The colours are applied as washes all over the area, with no attempt to shade—each area being completely covered by one colour. The type of colour used depends to a certain extent on the wood. In any case the colours should not normally be so opaque as to obscure the grain entirely. Water colour may be used on a light-coloured softwood, but a more penetrating stain or dye is better on harder woods. Oil stains are rather slow drying and may creep across a channel. Water stains may be bought as powders, which are dissolved in water. Spirit stains, bought ready-prepared or as powders for dissolving in methylated spirit, are quick drying. Aniline dyes will produce intense colours. A convenient form of dye is the "Mandarin" series of coloured waterproof drawing inks.

When the colouring is dry, the surface should be rubbed with a wax polish—either beeswax, or one of the prepared furniture polishes. This should be well worked in, in all directions, so that all of the incisions are filled with wax.

A step further than simply incising is to prepare a contrasting background to show up the incised pattern. The ground is not cut away, but is roughened to make a contrast with the pattern. The simplest way to roughen the background is to punch it. Steel punches can be bought with the ends cut in various stippled patterns. Alternatively, grooves can be filed across the end of a stout nail or iron rod (Fig. 10F). After the pattern is incised, the background is stamped down all over. The punch should be moved about and turned around, so that the background is a mass of dots, without any apparent pattern.

Punching is particularly suitable for intricate patterns, but the use of punches in carving is not usually considered good craftsmanship. It is better to achieve a similar effect by cutting grooves with a V tool. They may be all in the same direction, or the tool can be moved in many directions. In any case the grooves need only be quite shallow, but they should be very close together, and taken just up to the bordering incised lines in every instance.

If a pattern with a tooled or punched background is stained, the roughened ground will absorb more stain and appear darker, setting off the decoration rather like a silhouette—in fact silhouettes should be kept in mind when preparing designs for this treatment (Fig. 10G). Name boards and house numbers are also suitable subjects for this work (Fig. 10H). Colouring will give prominence where needed.

A different method of making name boards is to incise the lettering

(Fig. 11). A clean oak board, with a name incised, has a dignity and charm of its own. However, the very simplicity of the design calls for the choice of the right alphabet together with flawless workmanship, if the desired effect is to be achieved. A good Roman alphabet should be chosen. Several experimental layouts should be tried on paper. The spacing of letters should appear even—this does not mean that they are in fact the same distance apart. Letters with sloping sides need to be closer to their neighbours than letters with vertical sides. The letters will have moderate serifs (the points at the corners) and these should be enlarged to suit the carving technique. Great care should be taken in preparing the drawing of the lettering, as perfect carving will be wasted on bad setting out, or poor letter forms.

When a satisfactory layout has been drawn, it should be transferred to the wood. This can be done with carbon paper, but most of the lines should then be gone over with a sharp pencil. It may be preferable to draw the design afresh directly on the wood, so that you have fine and accurate lines to work from. All of these letters are cut in a somewhat similar way to chip carving, so that centre lines as well as outlines should be marked in. The angle between the sides of the cut should be about 60°, so choose a width that will give sufficient depth to produce good shadows and show up the lettering, but not so deep that carving becomes difficult and laborious. A few letters cut on scrap wood will give an idea of correct sizes for a particular purpose.

A V tool is useful, but it is not an easy tool to use, particularly when cutting the larger grooves, and as this work does not allow for discrepancies, the grooves are better cut with chisel and gouge in stages. A V tool cutting both sides at once is bound to be cutting against the grain on one side at some stages, with consequent roughness. By cutting the sides of the groove independently, a smoother result is possible.

The first step in incising lettering is to cut straight down on the centre lines. This can be done by cutting with a knife, but for the long

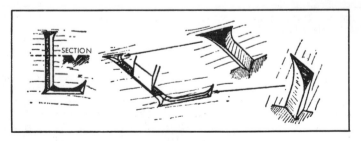

FIG. 11

straight cuts a wide chisel will produce a straighter result. Similarly, where a gouge of a suitable curve can be found, it can be used to cut in the curved centre lines. These cuts should be taken the full depth, using a mallet if necessary. Straight cuts will be even in depth, except for the serifs and other places where they blend into curves. Curves will be deepest where they are widest. Centre cuts of serifs will graduate from nothing at the corners to full depth at the centres.

Cutting away the slopes should be done deliberately—many little bites will not produce the clean finish desired. The bulk of the waste must be cut in one or two slices, then a clean paring with a fairly wide tool, from the outside line to the bottom of the centre cut. Be careful that in cutting down one side the chisel or gouge does not jump across and penetrate the other side. Watch the direction of the grain, and where the grain is diagonal to a cut, use the tool with a slightly slicing action in the direction of the grain. This will leave a smoother finish, as there is less tendency to bend or crush the fibres.

Cut all the major parts of the letters first. For the serifs, gouges may be used as far as possible, but some cutting may have to be done with a knife. Let the cuts of the serifs flow into the main cuts to leave a smooth change from curve to straight, or one curve to another. The cut surfaces should have a tool finish, and the temptation to use glass-paper resisted. Incised lettering loses its characteristic freshness if it is given any other treatment after carving.

It is often desirable to cut away parts of backgrounds completely, so that the main feature of the design is set off more prominently. Even the simple tool work so far described can be combined with piercing to produce badges and emblems on book ends (Fig. 12A), letter racks etc. Many of the old furniture designers combined piercing with carving, principally in chair backs. Chippendale usually included it in his designs. Many examples of old chests and cupboards with pierced carving, can be seen in the Victoria and Albert Museum. Many churches have elaborately carved and pierced screens. In this case the piercing serves the dual purpose of setting off the carving and allowing the congregation to see beyond. Of course, the tools used for piercing are also useful in cutting outlines and removing waste when tackling solid carving.

Piercing is done with a variety of saws, all with narrow blades, so that they can be guided around corners and curves. A hole is drilled, if it is a closed shape, and the saw threaded through. The choice of saw depends mainly on the thickness and hardness of the wood being worked. For wood up to about $\frac{3}{8}$ in. thick a fretsaw or jigsaw can be used. Fretsaw blades are graded by number, the coarsest being No. 6. The blade is kept tensioned by a spring steel frame, into which it is fitted with its teeth pointing towards the handle. A fretsaw is used while sitting, with the work supported on a V-cut in a sawing board (Fig. 12B). A smaller version of the frame, adjustable to take various

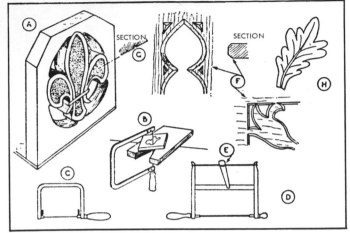

FIG. 12

lengths of blade, is called a piercing saw.

Where the wood is too tough or thick for cutting with a fretsaw, the slightly coarser coping saw (Fig. 12C) is used. This is probably the most useful saw in the series for wood carvers in any case. A coping saw blade is of the same type as a fretsaw, but it is thicker and coarser. It will cut thicker and harder wood, but cannot be used for such intricate work as a fretsaw. The edge left by a fretsaw is usually quite clean, but the edge left by a coping saw may need cleaning up. A coping saw may be used in the same way as a fretsaw, or the blade can be reversed so as to cut on the push stroke, and the work held vertically facing the worker, in a vice.

If wood thicker than about 1 inch has to be shaped, the tool to use is the bow saw (Fig. 12D). Blades are about 9 inches long and $\frac{1}{4}$ inch wide. Consequently, although they will cut thicker wood, they are mainly of use in roughing out a shape which is later worked to the exact outline by other tools. The blade should be kept under a strong tension by the lever (Fig. 12E) or screw at the top.

The amateur woodworker who has had some experience of fretwork will find that combining carving with it carries the job a stage further. A piece of fretwork alone seems flat and unfinished—artistically not satisfying. Many fretwork designs include leaves and floral decoration. These can be improved by the use of carving tools. Edges can be chamferred (Fig. 12F). Outlines can be carried through, where the design has to stop short because of constructional considerations

(Fig. 12G). Veins may be put in leaves (Fig. 12H) and a suggestion of detail given to flowers by the use of a V tool or small gouge. Eventually, of course, the craftsman will find that with the greater scope of carving, the fretwork becomes subsidiary to the work with carving tools, and not vice versa.

CHAPTER V

LOW RELIEF CARVING

HAVING reached this far and mastered the carving tools with a fair degree of control, the beginner will be feeling the urge to tackle something with more shape and needing treatment with a greater variety of tools. Gouges, in a variety of sizes and sweeps, are the most useful additions to the basic few tools. One or two spoon-bit gouges are useful for working in recesses, as when levelling backgrounds which are surrounded by higher parts. While almost any shape can be carved with very few gouges, it is easier to obtain a good finish with a choice from a larger selection. A fairly flat curve worked with a too-small gouge will inevitably be uneven, unless considerable care and patience is expended on it, but with a gouge of the right size and curvature a good result is easily and quickly obtained.

Patterns similar to those described for incising can be worked with a background more deeply recessed by the use of a gouge. The pattern is outlined with a V tool, or it can be followed around with a gouge having a quick curve (Fig. 13A). An alternative is to cut around a little distance from the line, leaving the final cutting to shape until after some of the background has been removed. The object of this type of carving is to throw the pattern into prominence by cutting away the background to a fair depth, leaving its surface usually rough in contrast to the design.

After cutting around the outline the background is cut down with a gouge having a fairly quick curve. A gouge with a deep curve is unlikely to tear out the wood as its corners will be kept above the surface. A shallow gouge may get its corners below the surface and start a split. Cutting away the background should be done systematically, using comparatively short scoops with the gouge (Fig. 13B). These should be of uniform depth, but the result should not be of too uniform appearance. No attempt should be made to get a perfectly flat recess. However, if the depth is about $\frac{1}{8}$ in. at one part it is wrong to be double this at another part. The hollows left from the gouge should all be of about the same size—so that no part of the background is over-conspicuous, and the attention is focused on the pattern.

For a shallow recess it is probably best to outline the pattern with a V tool and cut up to this carefully with a gouge. For deeper work the actual outline is cut to the line after most of the background has been cut out. This is done by paring with suitable gouges and chisels. They should be held slightly off of vertical to give a sloping cut (Fig. 13C). It is wrong to undercut for general work, as this weakens the edge as

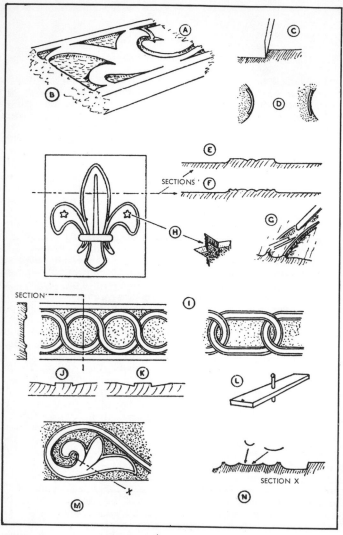

FIG. 13

well as not having such a good appearance. The exception is when the part has to appear to stand out, as a leaf curling upwards at the edge. Curves should be cut with gouges with sweeps as near as possible fitting the patterns. For an inside curve the sweep may be slightly less, and for an outside curve slightly more (Fig. 13D). Where the tool used for cutting in does not exactly fit the shape, it can be trued up with a slicing action, using either a knife or a skew-ended chisel.

Most designs with cut-away backgrounds are made more effective by tool work on the surface. An example is the fleur-de-lys or Scout Badge. In its simplest form (Fig. 13E), the strap and central spine are worked. They are outlined with a V tool, which need not cut very deeply. The strap and spine are rounded and the outside of the V cut is worked down to a shallow slope, blending into the surface.

For a more elaborate treatment of the same basic pattern, the outline is followed by a raised border (Fig. 13F). This is worked in the same way as the spine and strap, by marking with a V tool, then the edge of the border is left without further treatment and the inside blended into the surface. The top of the border is hollowed with a gouge having a fairly deep sweep. The safest way to obtain a good finish in this hollow is to cut away some of the waste at the centre by a slice with the gouge, then to trim away each side, varying the direction of the cut to suit the grain (Fig. 13G). The stars are sunk by cutting their outline with the V tool or small chisel, removing the waste with gouge and knife, and punching the background (Fig. 13H).

The hollow strapping pattern can be used in a number of designs, such as interlacing geometric figures, or the links of a chain (Fig. 13I). The design may be a panel or it can form part of the shaped edge of a book-end, cabinet side or similar piece. Designs may be built up as centre pieces or borders.

Where the hollow strappings cross in a design, the lower one should be bevelled away gradually (Fig. 13J); not with a sharp angle (Fig. 13K). Of course, this should be done as the next stage after outlining, before working the groove. If the pattern is at the edge of a piece of wood, the part away from the edge can be outlined, and the groundwork carved to blend into the surface. The groundwork inside the shapes need not be cut away very deeply, but it should be of an even depth. A simple depth gauge, consisting of a matchstick sliding in a hole in a block of wood (Fig. 13L), is useful for comparing depths.

Much relief carving is based on leaf forms. Quite often the design is conventionalized to such an extent that the carved leaf does not seem to have much in common with the natural article, but that is the privilege of the artist in wood—to take something and adapt it to suit his particular medium. The maple leaf (Fig. 14A) is a shape frequently used and modified in building up designs, and carving this in low relief is a good introduction to this sort of carving. Leaves from one tree in nature conform to a family shape, but differ in detail. In the same way

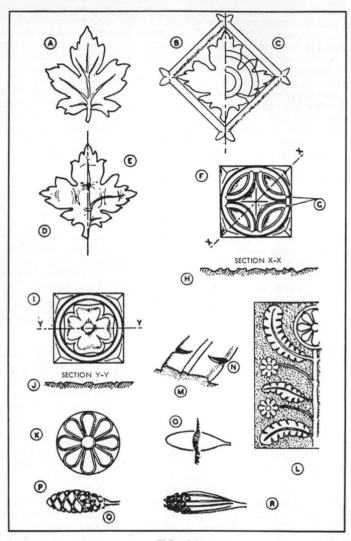

FIG. 14

leaves in a carved design need not be absolutely alike, but they should agree in the number of points etc.

To carve a sample leaf, choose a block of wood with a free-cutting grain and about 5 inches square. Sketch in the outline of the leaf with bold pencil lines. Set in the background by cutting with a V tool or gouge a square which encloses the leaf (Fig. 14B). Do not attempt to follow the outline at this stage. Cut away the background about $\frac{1}{4}$ in. or more, as depth is needed to allow the surface of the leaf to be carved, while it must still stand out from the ground. However, this must not be carried to excess, as shallow relief carving standing high above the background does not look right. The groundwork can be cut away within a border, or carried to the edge of the block.

The surface of the leaf is given a wavy appearance in a conventional manner by cutting curved grooves, so that there are undulations radiating from about the point where the veins of the leaf meet— just below the middle in this example. Draw in the curves with a pencil compass. Cut them in with a gouge having a medium sweep (Fig. 14C).

Cut in the outline of the leaf. Start with the deepest indentations, using gouges which fit the outline and cut away the groundwork to the same level as that outside. The edges of the parts of the leaf which appear curled up may be slightly undercut to increase the effect, but most of the edges should slope slightly the other way. Level all of the groundwork with a fairly flat gouge.

The next stage is to smooth out the curved gouge cuts to give the surface its smooth but undulating appearance. This is done with various gouges, cutting diagonally or with the grain. The hollows should not remain as parts of perfect circles, but should take a natural form on each lobe of the leaf (Fig. 14D).

The leaf may be left at this stage, but it will look more natural if veins are given to the main lobes. These should be drawn in then outlined with a small deep gouge, called a "veiner", if possible. Otherwise use a V tool. The vein should die out into nothing at the end (Fig. 14E). It will have square edges, which should be rounded off and the outside of the cut eased off into the surface of the leaf. To finish off the job the outside of the leaf should be given a very slight chamfer all round. This should be very small, and hardly apparent, but it reduces the risk of parts crumbling or chipping off.

Examples of low relief carving can be found in museums amongst domestic furniture of some 500 years ago. The country craftsman, with his limited equipment and comparatively narrow experience, drew on the designs he saw in churches and the larger houses, and simplified them to suit his tools and ability. The following carvings are on an oak cupboard of about 1500, in the Victoria and Albert Museum, London. They can be worked with two or three gouges, and can be adapted to suit modern pieces.

The doors are pierced, to ventilate the interior, using a design based on a popular shape of church window (Fig. 12F). The doors are also decorated by carvings enclosed in squares. Two designs are used— a geometric one (Fig. 14F) and a conventional flower (Fig. 14I). The geometric design is set out with compasses. The hollow strapping is worked with a gouge, as described earlier in this chapter—on a circle it is particularly necessary to cut away the waste at the centre of the groove, then trim each side to the line, to suit the direction of the grain. Where the strappings meet, the cuts should be of even depth and the hollows should make a clean mitre (Fig. 14G). The other hollows or pockets are cut out by chip carving methods. The central button should be left standing, with slightly convex sides (Fig. 14H).

The floral pattern is tackled in a very similar way to the maple leaf example. In drawing this, or any other pattern which consists of a motif repeated around a centre, only a part need be drawn on paper, then moved around when transferring it to the wood. Guide lines should be pencilled first. In this case a quarter drawing will be sufficient although with such a simple outline a half drawing gives a better idea of the finished appearance. Where the carver is uncertain of the final appearance and is unable to visualize the result of his cuts it is a good plan to take a hint from the sculptor and make a preliminary model in Plasticine or other modelling clay. This can be done for a simple flat relief carving if desired, but it is even more valuable when starting the carving of animal or human figures.

The flower is outlined with suitable gouges and chisels. Cut across the grain before cutting the lines laying with the grain. There is no need to go very deep—¼ in. is plenty on a pattern 5 inches square. Pare the background away with gouge cuts sloping down from the surface level. Outline the central button with a suitable gouge, to a depth of about ⅛ in. In preparing these designs it is a good plan to have the stock of gouges by you when making the drawing. Then such things as the curve of the button and the hollow outline of the petal can be made to suit the nearest gouge you possess.

Cut in the shape of the petal surface by paring towards the central button, being careful to restrain the gouge as it reaches the end of the cut (Fig. 14J). Curve the outside of the flower down towards the background. Trim the button to a uniform curve. The border is a hollow strapping with chip-carving similar to the geometric pattern.

Another conventional floral design has the petals cut with single hollow surfaces. To avoid thin edges, which might crumble, the edges of petals are left with a narrow flat surface (Fig. 14K). Each petal should be hollowed, gradually, then cleaned out to the finished shape with one sweep of the gouge. It is best to practise this cut on scrap wood. The gouge is entered nearly vertically and the hands dipped as the greatest width is reached. Further dipping reduces both the depth and width of the cut. Trials cuts will show the shape of hollow most suitable for a particular gouge, and the work will be simplified if this is used as the basic shape in preparing a design.

Old oak chests of the Middle Ages were often the only substantial possession of a family, and this solitary piece of furniture lent itself to decoration by carving. An example, from the year 1637, has panels carved with flowers of the type just described, together with leaves carved in a very similar way (Fig. 14L). The whole panel is about 12 in. × 9 in.

The leaves are roughly outlined, but without the deep indentations. The veins are cut and the sides of the leaf hollowed slightly towards the veins by lengthwise sweeps of a gouge (Fig. 14M). The outlines are then cut back to the line with cuts having a pronounced slope. This results in a V of chip-carved form in the leaf indentations (Fig. 14N). The background is sunk about ⅛ in. and punched all over.

Another thing frequently appearing on old chests is a pattern suggested by ears of corn. In its simplest form the outline of the ear is cut and the surface carved to a low curve (Fig. 14O). Diagonal lines are worked across the width with a V tool in both directions, so as to leave small diamonds (Fig. 14P). These diamonds are then shaped to form curved knobs representing the grains of corn (Fig. 14Q). Grain does not usually lay in straight lines in both directions, although the rows are more likely to be straight in line with the stalk than crosswise, so that an alternative way to simulate ears of grain is to cut grooves lengthwise, then carve the knobs individually along the lines, avoiding parallel rows crosswise (Fig. 14R). On some of the old chests the grain is carved on the ears so that lines are avoided in both directions. To do this, each knob of grain has to be carved individually.

Patterns can be built from interlacing straps combined with leaves. Borders can be made by repetition patterns. Letting the strap broaden into a three-part leaf is a common and effective design (Fig. 13M). In laying out these designs the general proportions should be indicated by free-flowing curves, before the details are put in.

The strapping broadens as it reaches the leaves, but the depth remains about the same. To do this, the cross-section changes from part of a circle to more oval. To get this effect, the bottom of the curve is cut with a flatter gouge than the sides (Fig. 13N). The parts of the leaf are hollowed in the same way, the centre of the broader parts being almost flat. There should be a border all round the leaves. This can be left flat, but it looks better if it is given a slight outward chamfer with a chisel or flat gouge.

CHAPTER VI

CONVENTIONAL RELIEF CARVING

CARVING differs from most forms of artistic expression in allowing the work to be three-dimensional, instead of two-dimensional only. A flat drawing has length and breadth, but to this carving adds depth. At first it may be difficult for anyone newly introduced to carving to appreciate this, as the work is viewed with a two-dimensional outlook, and the carving tackled as a picture on a flat surface. Of course, much carving can be described in this way and many of the projects so far described in this book have little depth, so that the result is still comparatively flat.

Carving of original figures or animals in deep relief calls for artistic ability, and the appreciation of shapes in the solid. Once the two-dimensional attitude is abandoned there is considerable satisfaction in carving in deep relief. Some of the most successful wood carvers favour a bold treatment, cutting away large pieces with each cut, risking an occasional mistake, and arguing that only in this way can the desired effect be produced. Probably some modification of this method is advisable, at least at first, but it is a fact that the too-cautious nibbling of tiny shavings is more likely to produce what amounts to a low relief carving, however much the background is cut away.

Not every carver is a skilled artist. While artistic ability is necessary to consistently produce the best original work, the less artistic carver, who is nevertheless skilled at handling tools, can produce some very satisfying work with rather different methods. Where the artist depends almost entirely on his eye, his less artistic colleague will use templates and measuring instruments to ensure faithful reproduction of his drawings, clay model or original example. Where the artist will prefer making panels showing scenes and figures as he visualizes them, the craftsman will prefer work of a more conventional character. Where the artist's accent will be on design, the craftsman will concentrate on execution. All carvers should have a knowledge of certain conventional forms in any case.

Leaves are frequently used, and they provide good examples for practice. Apart from the very conventional forms mentioned in the last chapter, leaves can be given a more natural appearance within the limits of the material. The simple form shown (Fig. 15A) is intended to have the effect of a fragile flexible leaf waving in the breeze. To this end, details of veins and surface markings are almost ignored and the accent is put on the undulations—which need not, of course, be exactly as shown, in fact if the form is used for a group of leaves the surface curves should differ between leaves.

Cut in the outline and sink the background in the usual way, then make bold gouge cuts across the surface where the deepest hollows are to come (Fig. 15B). They should radiate from near the stem as the ribs of the leaf stiffen it in that direction and deep curves across the lines of stiffness would be unnatural. From this point use flatter gouges to produce the final surface finish (Fig. 15C). The leaf will look more natural if it does not lie parallel with the background. One side may be higher than the other. Turning opposite sides up and down adds to the effect (section, Fig. 15A).

Carving in deeper relief calls for an understanding of the need to have parts in different planes, so that prominence is given to some parts, while others appear to pass under or behind them, giving an effect of perspective which is not usually as great as it seems. In the example (Fig. 15D) the shield may carry a monogram, while the leaves, of the privet type, radiate at different levels from behind it.

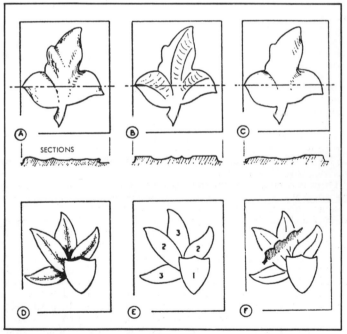

FIG. 15

After cutting in and sinking the background to a good depth the work is lowered to give the three working levels, before carving is commenced. The shield remains flat at the original surface of the wood, two leaves are lowered by about a third of the depth, and two others a further third (Fig. 15E, 1, 2, 3). The surfaces need not be parallel with the background—in general the perspective is improved if they are deeper where they appear to pass under another part. Shape the leaf surfaces by cutting down the centre with a V tool, then broaden this to make the sides of the leaf curve back from the centre (Fig. 15F). Overlapping parts may be slightly undercut. Be careful not to damage the lower surface when trimming the edge of an upper one.

The acanthus leaf is probably the most common of the conventional forms used in carving. Although based on a natural leaf originally, its usual carved form is very conventionalized. The design grew out of classic Greek architecture, being the pattern used on the capital of a Corinthian column. Carvers of the Renaissance Period adopted it, and it is still a popular carving design. Although there are many variations the characteristics are a bold treatment and the "eyes" between the main parts of the leaf.

A panel, which can later form the end of a book trough or other articles, should be tackled as an example to learn the usual form of this leaf. A piece of even-grained wood, say lime, sycamore or pine, about 8 in. × 6 in. × 1 in. should be chosen. Ease of cutting is an advantage at this stage, so the harder woods should be avoided.

The design should be drawn full-size on paper. Only half need be completed in detail. Basically, the design has a central stem and at each side two parts of the leaf, each divided into four lobes, with a curled over "pipe" finishing in an "eye" between the parts. The top of the stem broadens out into another curled over leaf part, filling the gap between the sides. In section the stem reaches the original surface, while the other parts fall away until the tips of the lobes almost reach the background (Fig. 16A).

There is no point in transferring all of the details of the drawing to the wood at first, as many of the lines would be cut off. Mark out from a centre line, turning the drawing over to ensure the work being symmetrical. At first draw only the main outline. The background is sunk about ⅜ in. and this may be gauged around the edges, if the panel is to be carved without a border. Cut around the outline with a deep gouge, keeping a short distance away from the line and ignoring the smaller inlets. With the same gouge, cut away the background from the edge towards the outline, working always diagonally across the grain and never letting the corners of the gouge go below the surface. Continue in this way almost down to the full depth, cutting in the general outline with gouges and chisels (Fig. 16B). Leave the finishing of the background until after the outline is finally shaped and the carving is almost complete, otherwise the background may become

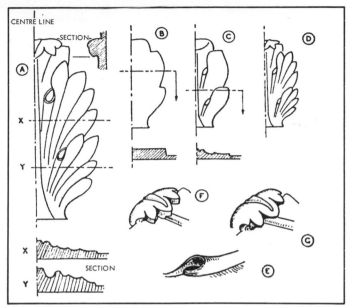

FIG. 16

marred by unintentional tool marks.

The two eyes at each side, with the pipes leading up to them, stand up almost to the original surface, but the parts of the leaf besides them sweep away to about ¼ in. above the background. This is the general shape, ignoring the shaping of individual lobes. The stem tapers from a short distance above its base to about half depth near the top. The next step is to mark in these parts and outline them with a veiner. The central stem is cut to its final lengthwise shape. The parts of the leaf beside the pipe are cut down to the general surface shape with a fairly flat gouge (Fig. 16C). Deepen the veiner cut at the edge of the pipe as necessary and cut the surface in a free-flowing curve to within about $\frac{1}{16}$ in. of the final depth. Cut away the bulk of the waste from other parts (under the top part, around the stem).

Draw in the exact outline. Cut this in to the full depth, cutting mostly vertically, but slightly under-cutting at the top to emphasize the rolled effect, and at overlapping parts to make them stand out. Take the background down to its final level with a very flat gouge.

Draw the lines which divide up the surface of the lobes (Fig. 16D). The lobes may have raised or hollow centres. In this case they are shown as hollows. The gouge cuts should flow in smooth curves. The pencil line should serve as a guide, but the cut must be made with an easy sweep, letting the tool slice smoothly, even if the curve followed is not exactly as originally drawn. A kink in a curve, due to trying to pull it back, will mar the work more than a sweet curve which does not go quite as was intended. The narrow ends of the grooves can be finished with a gouge cutting the complete width, but towards the ends a fairly flat gouge is needed at the bottom of the groove and a quicker one at the side. Watch the shape of the ridges between the lobes, as they are prominently concerned in the final effect of the carving.

Round the outside of the central stem and the pipes. The eyes should be cut in fairly deeply so as to make dark shadows. Cut vertically around their inner edges and remove the waste by cutting in at angle from the outer corner (Fig. 16E). The simplest treatment for the top is to form it very much like the other parts of the leaf, cutting vertically down at its outline where it lays over the rest of the design (Fig. 16F). It is more effective if undercut. Softwood may be too weak for this and in any case the undercutting should not be overdone. Before the top of the stem is finished, cut down vertically close to the outline of the top, then hollow this with gouges, letting the cut be deeper at the ends than the centre (Fig. 16G). Finally, cut the detail work on the edges.

All of this work will almost certainly have been done with the block of wood flat on the bench. Support it vertically so that the light comes diagonally from the side and examine it from a distance. Try this with the light from both sides. If the panel is to finally be above, on, or below the eye level, view it also from those angles. This inspection will almost certainly show up small blemishes, facets that need rounding off, or odd fibres still clinging in recesses, which had not been noticed while the wood was flat on the bench. A carving depends mainly for its effect on the way the light produces bright spots and shadows, and it is a good plan to always have a final careful inspection with side lighting.

No leaf in nature was ever like the classic form just described, and a rather freer treatment will be favoured for much carving. The parts of the leaf are still formed in the same way, and this can be regarded as a good basic pattern, but they are laid out in a more natural way (Fig. 17A).

Many leaves can be conventionalized to suit carving, and several examples have already been mentioned. Oak being frequently used for carving, it is fitting that the oak leaf should be often used as a basic form (Fig. 17B). The oak leaf is comparatively simple, with no fine points which would be weak in wood, and a surface with a central vein and a slightly curved front. A single leaf is not very decorative, but a cluster can be arranged to attractively fill a space, either a border (Fig. 17C) or a panel.

The method of cutting a cluster is very similar to the treatment of the

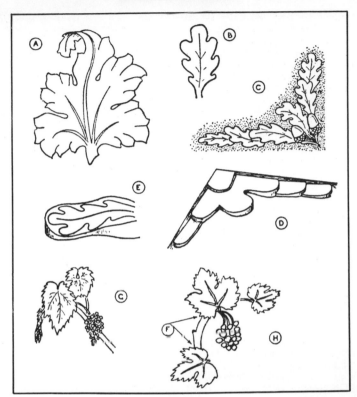

FIG. 17

acanthus leaf. The general outline is traced with a gouge and the background cut down. The lower parts of the design are then cut down in steps (Fig. 17D), so that the bulk of the waste is removed and the design is left in layers, each in the place it finally occupies. This preliminary roughing to shape, or "bosting in", should be the prelude to carving of any depth. It is a mistake to attempt detail work on one part before the general proportions are cut out.

The leaves should follow a natural curve, usually an ogee form (Fig. 17E) from base to point, but some may have the curve reversed, particularly where the raised tip might be weak. The leaves of the cluster are given their surface curve lengthwise, then the vein outlined and the curvature given the other way. The outline is cut in and the background levelled. In this type of carving the background may be worked as level and smooth as possible with flat gouges, or it can be given a rougher appearance by many small hollows made with a quick gouge or V tool. The rougher background shows up the carving, but with deep relief excessive contrast may be unnecessary.

The observant carver will find many examples of conventional leaf and foliage carving, which he can adapt to his needs. Any visit to an old house, church or museum will almost certainly show him specimens of interest. A sketch book will aid memory. Observance of nature will also suggest ideas. Pieces of actual foliage may be taken home and their shape and grouping adapted to a carved panel. In designing a carving consisting of foliage there are a few points to remember if the carving is to be a success.

Where the design includes a number of carved panels it is nearly always bad practice to design them so that the panels appear connected by branches, vines etc., going out of one panel and apparently continuing in the next, as though hidden behind the solid part of the framing. This is done in some Japanese work, but on the whole it tends to upset the solid appearance of the piece. Branches and stalks have to appear in a cluster. They may run to a border, if there is no adjoining panel, but quite often it is possible to arrange for them to disappear behind a leaf (Fig. 17F).

Natural clusters are most unlikely to conform to a set space. Their perspective too, is likely to be too deep for carving naturally. With a space to fill, the spray giving the original idea (Fig. 17G) has to be adapted to give a balanced appearance and to look right in the comparatively shallow depth (Fig. 17H).

Heraldry can provide many examples for the wood carver. The various figures and symbols used in heraldry lend themselves to carving. Old houses, castles and churches usually contain coats-of-arms and other heraldic devices, either in wood or stone, and these can be adapted as patterns, or the carver can use his imagination and devise a coat-of-arms or shield for school or club. The carving may be confined to the surround of the shield, and be in the form of foliage, supporting figures, crowns or scrolls with incised lettering. Colour plays a large part in heraldry, so that with a heavily carved surround, a plain shield with a brightly painted design can be very effective. Alternatively the design on the shield can also be carved, either painted or unpainted.

In the making of shields the carver can find something to suit himself, whatever his degree of skill at artistry or craftsmanship. A complicated design including unicorns and lions will tax the skill of the finest carver. At the other extreme the less-experienced carver can confine his work to simpler emblems and produce a quite effective result.

As a coat-of-arms was first used in the days of body armour, the basis is usually a shield shape, and this was usually surmounted by a helmet of some sort. The knight, fully clothed in armour, had a plume or other drapery flowing from his helmet for easy identification, so that in planning a design it is safe to arrange the surrounding carving in a form which has its main lines radiating from the vicinity of the helmet (Fig. 18A). The motto, or other inscription, fills the bottom on a scroll (Fig. 18B).

Pictures of armour, or actual examples sketched in a museum, offer a number of different helmet designs. A few are shown (Fig. 18C). The surrounding decoration can be in the form of foliage. Leaves of the acanthus type are not as suitable as something based on the laurel, with its more slender flowing lines (Fig. 18D). The effect is improved if the leaves overlap the shield slightly in a natural way at one or two points. While the two sides should have a balanced appearance, there is no need for one side to be an exact mirror reproduction of the other.

Leaves are not the only form of decoration. A long streamer, with swallow-tailed ends, can be twisted around as if unwinding or blowing in the breeze (Fig. 18E). This design can be drawn after twisting an actual ribbon or tape as an example, so as to observe the natural twists. The scroll at the bottom can be designed in the same way. The lettering on it may be incised, or the background can be cut down to leave the letters standing within a border.

A helmet has no flat surfaces, so that in carving it every part must be shaped to give the rounded effect and avoid any flat picture appearance. The carved helmet will usually be flatter in relation to its width than the actual helmet, but most cross-sections will be approximately elliptical. Many helmets have an angle at the front (Fig. 18Γ), and the inclusion of this helps to destroy any flat appearance. The main parts of the helmet may curve right down to the background, but any crosses or spikes on a crown should be cut vertically, or even undercut, to make them stand out in contrast.

The carving of leaves has already been covered. In carving a streamer the aim must be to give a free-flowing effect. To do this, the parts must be at different levels, and the surface of the ribbon should be curved, both in its length and width (Fig. 18G). Cut away the background by outlining with a gouge or V tool, and paring with a gouge. Cut in the outline. Treat the over-lapping parts carefully and pare the surface to give an undulating effect in the length of the ribbon and sufficient depth at the crossing for the upper part to stand out. Hollow the surface with a very flat gouge. An effect of thickness and twisting of the ribbon is given by taking off one edge at an angle (Fig. 18H), while undercutting the other slightly.

The scrollwork carrying the lettering is cut in the same way, but the actual surface on which the words are cut may be flat, each part curving away outside the lettering. The sharp twists are made to appear deeper than they actually are by setting them back from the outer surface and

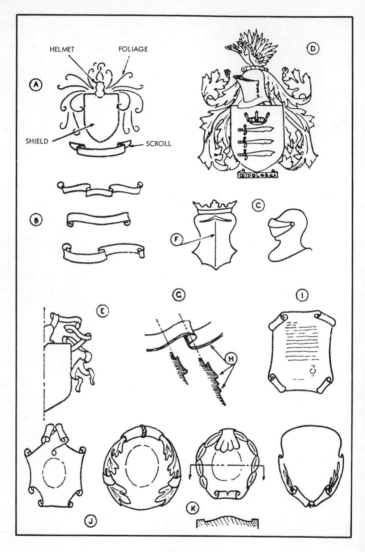

FIG. 18

undercutting the overlapping edges, so that shadows are formed. While the lower folds should be well back from the front, they should still be far enough above the level of the background to stand out from it.

Rather similar to the shield is the scroll or cartouche. This is a formal reproduction in wood of the effect of a piece of parchment curled at the edges (Fig. 18I). It serves as a centre piece to a carving, bearing initials, or arranged alone rather as a shield, for use as a trophy or independent decoration. From the simple parchment form it has developed to include formal leaves, swags of flowers and fruit, or completely departed from the parchment original and taken the shape of a shell.

The edge decoration is right up to the edge and in some cases the central surface flows right up the edge (Fig. 18J). This sort of cutting is best done by leaving the final trimming of the outside edge until the surface carving is complete. This ensures a smooth flow of the surface cuts and a crisp edge when the outline is finally cut.

The effect of the centre area will be spoilt if it is kept flat. The central part should be raised and its immediate surround fall away to disappear under the border (Fig. 18K). If the central area is to carry a monogram or initials, then the letters should be outlined and the surface further lowered. The finish should be a smooth tooled one, which will contrast with the raised letters and the finer carving at the edges.

The arrangements of leaves and foliage are carved by the methods already described. The rolled scroll edges need a different approach. Wood has to be kept to thicker sections than the original parchment, but the effect of the roll or curl should be as realistic as possible. The curl is exposed at one end, the edge going round in an easy curve, the effect of overlap being given by undercutting the overlapping edges. In most cases the opposite end is merely curved and slightly undercut. Cutting the open scroll end is very similar to the work described for linenfold designs (Fig. 19). The effect of old and cracked parchment is further given by making the edges slightly hollow, with odd tool marks to simulate cracks.

Linenfold designs (Fig. 19A, B, C) were developed in the Tudor period—the idea coming from the way the altar cloth was folded. In a conventionalized form the wood is carved to give the effect of cloth folded back on itself at several places. Besides its use in church furniture, linenfold patterns have been used on chests, bed-ends, drawer fronts and other items of household furniture. Usually the linenfold design is carved on a panel, fitted into the framework of the structure. For obvious reasons, the grain should run the length of the folds.

Cloth may be folded on itself to produce most intricate folds, and carvers have shown their skill by reproducing them. Normally the design of a panel is kept symmetrical by letting the cloth come to a ridge at the centre. A design with simple folds will illustrate the method of working. A start should be made by making a drawing, showing at least one quarter of the panel, both in front and end views.

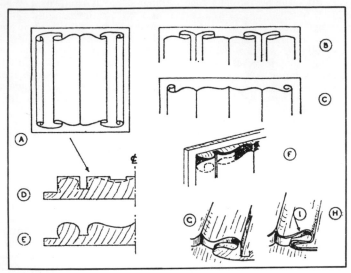

FIG. 19

The first step in carving is to cut away the background all round. As this is straight, the simplest method is to use a fillister plane. If the panel is $\frac{3}{4}$ in. thick the ground should be reduced by about $\frac{1}{4}$ in. Most of the lengthwise work may be done with planes. Draw the end shape on the wood and cut grooves in the waste part with a plough plane (Fig. 19D). From this stage use hollows and rounds or other suitable moulding planes, to bring the wood to the right section (Fig. 19E). These tools will do most of the shaping, but undercutting of rolls will have to be done with carving tools. The final smoothing of the surface should be done with glasspaper held over shaped blocks of wood, but this treatment should be left until after the ends are carved, as minute particles of glass left on the work will blunt the carving tools.

The opposite ends are carved in the same way, and the drawing is needed as a guide, otherwise there is a risk of cutting some part away at the wrong level. If the background has been cut straight across with a plane, the next step is to cut the outline of the folds with gouges and chisels, removing the shaded part (Fig. 19F).

The outline giving the second fold is traced with a gouge cut, the waste removed by cutting down to a pencilled line on the end, and the overlapping edge pared vertically (Fig. 19G). The outline of the bottom fold is pencilled on this new surface and cut out in the same way, so that it blends into the lengthwise groove (Fig. 19H). The lowest part of the bottom fold should stand sufficiently proud of the background for its outline to show up clearly.

To emphasise the folded linen effect the overlapping parts are undercut, but the sharper curves as the cloth changes from one surface to the next are allowed to follow round in an unbroken line of about $\frac{1}{8}$ in. or less in width (depending on the size of the panel). This undercutting deepens the shadows and makes the upper parts stand out. The line of the curves is followed around the edge of the broad surfaces by a chamfer of the same width (Fig. 19I).

There is a fascination about linenfold work, and an examination of work in churches or on antique furniture will show its beauty and effectiveness. Once the method has been mastered on simple folds, complications can be introduced—creases between the folds, and curled over edges.

CHAPTER VII

FIGURE RELIEF CARVING

THE carving of conventional forms in various degrees of relief provides plenty of opportunity for the exercise of skill in tool handling, and a certain amount of artistic expression; although the worker with little artistic ability can do this work on a par with that of his more artistic colleague, providing he follows prepared designs. If, however, figures of animals, birds or human beings are to be included in a piece of carving in any but a strictly conventional manner, artistic ability is necessary if the result is to be satisfactory. Figure carving needs initiative and individual interpretation—it is difficult to prepare a design on paper that can include every little shape and facet that go to make up a truly lifelike figure carving. An appreciation of curves and lines, together with sufficient confidence to make bold cuts to transfer them to the wood, are some of the qualities making for success in figure carving.

A start is best made by choosing a single figure with a fairly plain outline and a smooth surface (Fig. 20A). The detail work in faces or feathers, for instance, should be left until later. A smooth-skinned animal or a man in plain armour, are easier than a bird or a lady in an elaborate dress, although birds and similar figures can be rendered quite attractively, without attempting to copy the texture of their covering.

The design chosen may be cut on a block with the background cut away to the edge, so that the finished piece may be enclosed in a separate framing, or the block itself may be carved to frame the figure. For this treatment the block should be fairly stout. For an overall size of about 12 in. by 10 in. it could be about $1\frac{1}{2}$ in. thick. The background is cut away to nearly an inch, while the border is cut back about $\frac{1}{2}$ in., allowing the figure to stand forward of the border with a fair depth above the background to allow of good shaping (Fig. 20B). The border may carry lettering or scrollwork, depending on the use of the final panel, but for most purposes an arrangement of foliage would be out of place.

A preliminary drawing should be made on paper, and the main outline of the figure only transferred to the wood at first. The first cuts will be to lower the background to the level of the border. The figure is outlined with a small gouge. It will probably be safer to go around outside this with a deeper gouge before chopping away the background to a gauged line on the edge. As the depth increases and the first gouged outlining is passed, the edge of the figure is set in by cutting down at an angle. Most of the chopping to depth should be done by cutting diagonally across the grain.

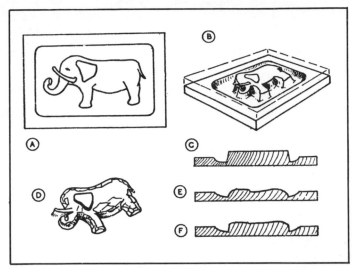

FIG. 20

As the border level is reached, use a gouge with a very flat sweep to level off the border, if it is to remain uncarved. Draw the shape of the inner edge of the border. Set in the outline of the figure deeper and cut inwards towards this from the border with a large gouge, so that the final background is saucer-shaped (Fig. 20C).

Other details on the figure can be drawn in as necessary. True up the outline as required, then proceed to bost in the general shape of the figure with a gouge. The object of this is to reduce the carving to something approaching its final shape, so that the actual finishing cuts are comparatively light. The parts with deepest relief should be cut first, e.g. the offside legs of four-legged animals. It is at this stage that the value of artistic appreciation of shape will first be felt (Fig. 20D). See that the various levels are in the right relationship with each other.

With the general proportions settled, other work consists in finishing parts to shape with appropriate tools. Be careful to let curves flow freely—a kink or bump in a line will be obvious to every viewer. Sharp tools, used boldly should guarantee good curves. Avoid flatness—nature does not include many level surfaces, so let all parts of an animal's body be curved, however slightly. Make full use of the depth, letting the curves go right down to the background (Fig. 20E). Shallow carving above a deep background looks wrong (Fig. 20F).

The final piece should show cleanly tooled surfaces, with no stray fibres still clinging in recesses. It is wrong to clean up with glasspaper. Before pronouncing the work complete, examine it held vertically with side lighting, or in the attitude and with the lighting it will finally experience if it is to be in a permanent position.

For success in carving figures or animals, whether in relief or in the round it is necessary to know something of anatomy and to study animals at every opportunity. Photographs and pictures will be a help, but they cannot tell everything, and a brief but methodical study of the actual animal will be of more use than a large number of pictures. It is the observation of shape in three dimensions which is valuable. A note should be made of sectional shapes—either mentally or on paper. Sketches made on the spot can be quite simple, providing they serve to remind you of some point. Things to watch are the location and setting of eyes; the proportion between head, legs and body; lumps and hollows, particularly those which vary as the animal sits or stands, and your estimate of cross-sections through parts of the animal.

A clay model may be useful in arriving at general proportions, but a sketch showing the main outline and features should be all the guidance needed in addition to the stored-up mental images of the animal, and the carver's idea of the final shape.

There have been many carvings consisting of animals treated naturally but worked into formal designs of tracery, foliage etc. Many examples of this sort can be found in churches. Ends of pews, choir stalls and similar places give the carver a chance of showing his skill over a fairly large area. As there were usually several similar areas in the church, the carving is repeated in general form, but differing in detail. An examination of such pews will show the would-be carver how the skilled craftsman of former years used wood with its characteristics and limitations to take the form of an animal or bird.

In the larger churches, abbeys and cathedrals, the underside of the choir and clergy seats can provide plenty of interest for the wood carver. Where the seats are arranged to hinge up and the clergy had to stand for long parts of the service, a block on the underside was arranged in a position to give some support. These miserere or misericord seats appear to have been places where the carver was given a fairly free hand to decorate in any way he chose. The result is a selection of carvings, some grotesque but mostly humorous, and some satirical in relation to the events of the carver's day. Sometimes the technique is far from good, but the artistic effect and the portrayal of the craftsman's intention is more important. Many of these carvings are worth sketching or photographing, and the ideas developed in the carver's modern work.

CHAPTER VIII

WOOD SCULPTURE

CARVING figures in deep relief calls for an appreciation of shape in three dimensions, although the third dimension is usually in reduced proportions. Carving in the round carries the process to its logical conclusion—the carving stands alone, without a surrounding background, and should look right when viewed from any angle. This means that any thought of pictorial representation should be put aside, and the imagination concentrated on true shape in all directions. This is easier for some than others. Not every carver will aspire to sculpture, and those who do will have little use for written instructions, but will depend on their own artistic sense.

Once an appreciation of the characteristics of the wood is mastered, and the worker is proficient in the use of carving tools, there is not much that a book can tell him. There can be a few pointers to method, but success is mainly a matter of artistic expression. In this sort of carving, good form is more important than technique. The best carver technically may get his satisfaction out of carving conventional forms. The best carver artistically will prefer sculpture.

Sketches are important in the first stages, and from these a skilled carver might go ahead and carve his figure, having visualized the appearance and dimensions in all directions. It is an ideal to aim at, but the beginner is better advised to model his figure in clay or Plasticine first. This will ensure that he gets the shape he wants, and will be a guide to what parts to cut away. The clay model can be much smaller and need not be finished. Once it has served its purpose as a guide to the main proportions it should be discarded. It is wrong to slavishly copy a model—the hands and tools should be following what is visualized by the mind.

The sketches should be at least two, giving the front and side views (Fig. 21A) as the work will almost certainly start as a squared block. The drawings may be on paper, but should be full-size. Proportions should be kept thin. What looks too thin in the flat, will appear thicker in the round. Transfer the side view to two opposite surfaces of the block (Fig. 21B). Cut away the waste shown by the side view. This may be done with a band saw, bow saw, or by chopping with a gouge, depending on the particular job. Do not cut out openings in the design.

When the shape is correct in one direction, mark out the shape in the other view at right angles to it. The surface is no longer flat, so that most of the drawing will have to be done freehand, with the paper drawing as a guide. Cut out the waste in this direction in the same way as the first

61

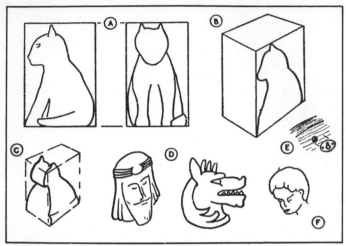

FIG. 21

(Fig. 21C). Up to this point the block will be held in any way convenient for cutting, but for carving it will probably be best to mount it upright, depending on the chosen figure. For most things, screwing to a turntable on the bench will be the best arrangement.

At this stage the outline is correct in two directions only and most parts are square in section. The next step is bosting in to get the figure into the correct general shape by removing the bulk of the waste wood. This is done by chopping with a mallet and a fairly large gouge. We now leave the point where drawings can be of much use. The clay model can be consulted for the main cuts, but we soon reach a point where we are dependent on our imagination, assessing the effect of proposed cuts on the actual job. It is as well to avoid too much timidity. It is natural to be afraid that a part will be spoilt by rash cutting, but a certain boldness is necessary if a worthwhile result is to be achieved. Bosting in should leave the figure approximately to shape, but with large gouge cuts mostly across the grain, all over it. The only part which might be left oversize at this stage is the base, where it is screwed to the turntable, and additional wood might be necessary to give a strong joint.

Cutting away large amounts is best done with a large gouge, chopping across the grain, usually with both points of the gouge projecting above the surface. Sometimes only one point need project, as when cutting a slope across the grain, and any split developing will go into the waste part. If a tool jams in the wood, do not hit it sideways, as this may split the wood or break the tool (hardened steel is rather brittle). Cut around it with another tool, until it loosens and falls out.

Guide lines may be pencilled on as required, marking such things as the centre of a face or location of an opening. Follow the bosting in with shaping the parts with tools which leave a smoother and more accurate surface. Where a space comes, as between legs, holes can be drilled through and the shape chopped out around them. In some cases a keyhole saw will be useful.

Points to watch include any evidence of squareness remaining. There should certainly be nothing to show that the work started as a square block. The work should appear as a whole—features should not appear to be applied, they should blend into the whole figure. The finish given, whether tools marks are prominent or smoothed out, and the amount of detail included, depend on the individual treatment. A carving of this type is a work of art, not one of several similar things, worked slavishly to a pattern.

Carving a large figure is an ambitious project as well as being rather costly. Carving the same thing in a smaller version can be tedious and some parts may have to be omitted due to their small size, unless the carver is an enthusiast for miniature work. An alternative, offering somewhat similar work, is the carving of masks or plaques, gargoyles or grotesque heads.

A plaque or mask will normally have its third dimension rather flattened, but otherwise can be regarded as a sort of solid carving with a flattened back. A normal face, without any accented features, is not easy to reproduce. Something with headgear, beard or a form which amounts almost to a cartoon is a better subject (Fig. 21D). The work can be based on a photograph or drawing, the imagination providing the other dimensions. Hanging can be arranged unobtrusively by a plate over a hole in the back (Fig. 21E).

Much early carving included the forming of heads, usually built into some supporting structure in the form of a bracket. The head might be that of an angel or child with wings, or a grotesque animal or gargoyle. Castles and church buildings of the Tudor period, for instance, will show the frequent use of child's heads in the pediments and brackets of the roof structure. Grotesque heads were used at many times, and may be found in more domestic woodwork, such as mantelpieces or over windows, as well as in the larger buildings where this might be expected.

Carving a lifelike adult head in wood calls for considerable skill and artistic ability, but a child's head can be worked effectively, providing simple rules are observed. A grotesque head, which is a form of cartoon with the features exaggerated possibly to fantastic lengths, will tolerate alterations and discrepancies, without them being apparent.

A knowledge of anatomy is valuable. Even when carving an exaggerated head, the basic structure should be kept in mind—the skull with its attendant muscles and tissues, even in a fantastic head, should have a feasible part in the construction. There is no real place in a book on carving for a discourse on anatomy, so the carver who is attracted by heads and figures, should read a simple book on anatomy so that his work starts on a sound foundation.

A child's head differs from an adult's in many ways. It is the incorporation of these rather pronounced differences that make the carving of a child's head more simple. Wood is not suitable for very fine detail, and it is the suggestion of general form which achieves the effect. In relation to the size of the head, a child's face is much smaller than an adult's. The upper part of the skull, particularly the forehead, is much more obvious and more forward than in most adults. A young child's features are well rounded and plump. Lips project and are pursed (Fig. 21F).

A clay model will be a help in getting correct proportions for a child's head. Experiments can be made and clay removed or replaced until a satisfactory appearance is obtained. Remember that the wood will not have the soft appearance and quality of surface that is obtainable on clay. Aim at general proportions. Too small a head is inadvisable for a first project—a 6 inch cube is about right. Treatment will be very similar to that described for figure carving earlier in this chapter. Draw the shape when viewed in one direction and cut this out. Draw the main outline as viewed at right-angles to the first, and cut this out. With the clay model or your imagination as a guide, bost in so that the general proportions are correct and the bulk of the waste wood is removed.

Much of the finishing work must be done without a mallet. Spade chisels and gouges are convenient for the more delicate work, but plain tools will deal with most of it. Too much detail should not be included. The art is in using sufficient lines and cuts to suggest the natural appearance without overdoing it. Hair is perhaps best indicated in outline, with waves shaped and a few cuts to indicate the outline of locks.

Gargoyles and grotesque heads may have had symbolic and superstitious meanings, but more often now they are the result of the carver's imagination. As already said, general effects are better than subtle expressions. Without the need for following nature closely, expressions can be exaggerated. In a laugh, the mouth may be said to split the face from ear to ear—in a grotesque carving the worker can let it actually do this. Wide open eyes show surprise or horror. The brows creased over the eyes show anger.

The next step after exaggerating human features while still letting them have a semblance of reality, is to add unnatural things, like hair or beards which terminate in leaves, or ears which are more like bat's wings. Human faces or expressions can be put on animals' heads. The Elizabethans produced many fantastic heads as items in their roof trusses and other parts of wooden structures. Hammer beam roofs with their angular structure gave the carver an opportunity of exercising his skill in a prominent position. All sorts of heads, from angels to the most fantastic inventions are found at the angles of the roof trusses.

The carver with an interest in grotesques will find other examples in ecclesiastical and civic carvings. The combination of human and animal forms, or creatures combining animal and bird forms, often appear. Such creatures occur in legends. Others are symbolic, intended to indicate something with the qualities or characteristics of two or more creatures.

Other examples of grotesques occur amongst native carvings. The Red Indian's totem pole is based on one or more fantastic figures. Natives all over the world use carving, often for religious or symbolic purposes. Quite often the work is very skilful, yet the tools are quite primitive. The carver looking for ideas for grotesques will find many amongst the work of native craftsmen.

CHAPTER IX

CARVING AND TURNING

THE craftsman who can combine wood carving with wood turning enlarges his scope considerably. A piece of furniture can be made to include parts which have been worked on the lathe, while other parts have been decorated by carving. Suggestions for that type of work are given later in the book, but this chapter deals with combinations of carving and turning in the same piece of wood.

A common combination is the fluting or scalloping of a turn piece. Usually the turning stage is finished completely and the work removed from the lathe before carving is commenced. It is possible for the carver without a lathe to buy ready-made turned pieces which he can improve by work with his gouges and chisels. With the work removed from the lathe, holding devices will usually have to be improvised, as the round section does not lend itself to holding by simply squeezing in a vice—cuts may be damaged or the work pressed out of round.

With a simple woodworking lathe the work will have to be removed for carving, but a lathe also intended for metalwork may have devices making it convenient as a holding arrangement while carving. If the headstock is equipped with a dividing attachment, that will provide the most accurate means of setting out flutes or other cuts evenly around the circumference. If the headstock has a chuck, the wood can be held by this and the back centre while carving. If it only has a prong centre, this is unlikely to stand up to the load while carving, and the work is better removed. Most carving of turned work involves even spacing around the work, and whether the dividing is done by the lathe dividing attachment or as described below, the marking of lines along a curved surface is very conveniently done with a pencil on a block of wood (Fig. 22A), while the article is supported by the lathe centres.

Flutes on a parallel or straight tapered turning are most easily marked out and carved (Fig. 22B). To mark out, obtain the length of the circumference (at both ends if it is a taper) by wrapping a strip of paper around marking or pricking through the overlap. Straighten out the paper and divide the circumference into the desired number and size of flutes. The work is simplified if the widths of flutes suit gouges you possess and the spaces between the flutes are the same width as the flutes.

If the spacings are marked on the edge of the paper, it can be wrapped around the wood and the marks transferred by pencil. Lengthwise lines are drawn with the aid of a rule.

If the work cannot be held by the lathe, it may be possible to hold it

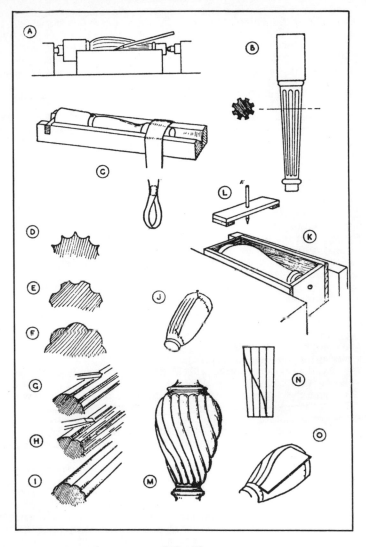

FIG. 22

in the vice, if the jaws are suitably padded. Another holding device is shown (Fig. 22C). This is a long trough, with a stop at one end which can be held in the vice or fixed to the top of a bench. The work is held by a strip of canvas or webbing fastened to one side of the trough and held down by foot pressure in a loop. An advantage of this arrangement is in the speed with which the position of the work can be altered, by merely relaxing the foot pressure.

Once the marking out and holding are satisfactory, the actual carving is fairly easy. In the case of parallel work, the curve of the end of the flutes is cut in by pressing down vertically with a suitable gouge. The angle of the gouge is then lowered and the flute cut carefully between the guide lines. A gouge with a medium curve is usually best. Too shallow a curve does not produce a flute deep enough to give sufficient light and shade to show the work to advantage, while a very deep flute has a rather coarse appearance and is more difficult to execute cleanly. If the grain is difficult, the centre of each flute should be cut with a small gouge, then the sides worked with the final gouge, operating in opposite directions if necessary, to avoid tearing up any grain.

If the fluting is tapered, the ends are cut in lightly with two different gouges, then the wood cut away with gouges of varying curves if the taper is sharp. With the commoner, more moderate tapers one gouge can usually go right through, the depth (and automatically the width) being reduced gradually towards the small end. There is less risk of tearing out grain on a taper, as cutting from the thick to the thin end is slightly diagonally across the grain, if this is straight.

Fluting may be done so that the flutes meet (Fig. 22D) instead of being spaced by plain wood (Fig. 22E), but it is difficult to keep the sharp edge between the flutes level and straight. If the whole surface is to be ridged, scalloping or nulling (Fig. 22F) is to be preferred. This is marked out in a similar way to fluting, without spacings.

Most of the work is done with a chisel. The lines are cut in with a knife or V tool (Fig. 22G), then the V broadened by chiselling (Fig. 22H), and the angles removed to produce the rounded sections (Fig. 22I). Most carved work should not be touched by glasspaper, but fluting or scalloping of turned work can be levelled by rubbing with glasspaper held around suitably-shaped blocks of wood. Care should be taken not to rub off the angles—which will happen if glasspaper is held loosely in the hand.

Where the fluting has to be done on a curved or bulbous turning, marking out is a little more difficult. Spacing around the work is done with strips of paper in the same way as with straight work. It may then be possible to mount the work in the lathe again and use a pencil on a block of wood (Fig. 22A). A piece of cotton stretched between pins (Fig. 22J) is a little tedious. As the shaped work is likely to be difficult to hold while carving, a jig can be made to hold it, and this can also be used for marking out.

The jig is box-shaped, just large enough to clear the turning, which is held by its centres with screws at each end (Fig. 22K). The whole thing can be held in the vice, and may be stiff enough to resist turning while carving, or a thin wedge can be forced between the work and the jig at one end to lock it.

When the ends of the flutes or scallops are marked out, the lengthwise lines can be drawn with a gauge working on the jig. This is a strip with two guide blocks and a hole in which fits a pencil with sufficient freedom to move up and down as it follows the curve of the work (Fig. 22L). Working on a curved surface requires more care than on a straight one, but otherwise the carving is the same. Follow the grain, by cutting from the high parts to the low (in most cases), and not vice versa.

Carving on bulb or vase shaped turnings may have a spiral effect, without going so far round as to be called twist turnings. This is an interesting job for the wood carver (Fig. 22M). Of course, marking out is more difficult. The top and bottom are divided into the same number of equal spaces, as for straight fluting. The amount of twist is governed by the number of points around from that one vertically under a top one, the line is taken (Fig. 22N). As the distance around will vary with the length and number of flutes, experiments must be made with pins and string. The best effect is usually obtained when the angle of slope is about 30° to the centre line of the wood at the middle of the spiral.

The line given by a string is a regular spiral (or more strictly a "helix"). This can be used and all the lines marked out with pin and string, but the effect is probably more pleasing if the lines curve towards the lengthwise direction at the ends. One flute or scallop should be drawn in freehand to give this effect. When a satisfactory shape is obtained, it can be traced on a piece of paper bent over the turning. From this tracing a card template is made, and this is moved around from point to point in turn and the curve repeated at each place by drawing along the edge (Fig. 22O).

Carving involves careful watching of grain direction. For the most uniform results the same stage on each line should be done in turn before moving to the next stage. If a pair of bulbous carvings will form legs or pillars, the spirals should be in opposite directions. So that they match, the same template should be used, turned over.

One of the most intriguing combinations of carving and turning is the twist leg. This can be machine-made, and the twist legs on commercially-produced furniture are rapidly manufactured on a lathe with a rotating blade which gouges out the hollows. Machine-made twists cannot equal hand-worked ones, as there are limitations in the mechanical carving action.

The twist is somewhat similar to a screw thread. It may have one, two or three parts, in the same way that a screw may be a one, two or three start thread. It has a pitch, i.e. the distance from the top of one thread to the top of the next.

In planning a twist leg the important considerations are the pitch and the depth of the twist. As we are working in wood, with a grain stronger in one direction than the other, strength must be assessed alongside appearance. A leg with a short pitch, so that the thread goes round the wood many times in a given distance, will have much "short" grain, which is liable to crack under a load. At the other extreme a long pitch will have great strength, but a not very pleasing appearance. The depth of the thread also affects the strength. It is possible to work the hollows halfway or more through the wood, which may be considered attractive, but the grain will again be short and the structure weak. Obviously, the answer is a moderate twist and a moderate depth between the parts. In most woods, a single twist with a pitch about the same as the diameter, gives a satisfactory shape.

For a first attempt, a single twist should be chosen. This could form the stem for a candlestick or something similar. The object should be turned, with the part to be twisted left parallel. It is a convenience in working to avoid any parts of larger diameter at the ends, so that a complex turning to include a twist might be built up, with the twisted column turned with dowels to fit the other parts. Making a twist on a part of a large turning is not impossible, but for the first attempt a plain stem is easier. The twist may blend into the ends or a hollow can be turned at its extremities (Fig. 23A).

Divide the circumference into four and draw lines along. Draw lines around at distances corresponding to the pitch. This is most conveniently done with a pencil while the work is revolving in the lathe. The pitch need only be approximately the same as the diameter, and can be varied to give an equal spacing in the overall length. If the pitch circles have to be marked out without the help of a lathe, a strip of card can be bent around and the lines drawn along its edge.

There are several possible ways of marking out the twist. The first line to be drawn is the one following the top or apex of the thread (Fig. 23B—1st). This is not difficult to do freehand. Starting at one crossing, the line has to completely circle the wood to the next crossing of the same straight line with a pitch circle. It therefore crosses the other three lines at one-quarter, half and three-quarters of the distance. If these points are marked, it is fairly easy to join them up freehand (Fig. 23B). This is followed in the same way to the end of the twist.

Pins and thread can be used, the lines marked on the wood being used to check that the thread follows an even course before the line is drawn (Fig. 23C). A thin piece of card provides a better edge for drawing (Fig. 23D), but it may not lie flat, due to the spiral. Another way of using card, which will reduce the amount of preliminary marking out, is to cut a triangle, with its base equal to the circumference and height equal to the pitch. Wrapped around the rod, this gives a steady edge for drawing against (Fig. 23E).

Two other lines have to be marked each side of the first. These

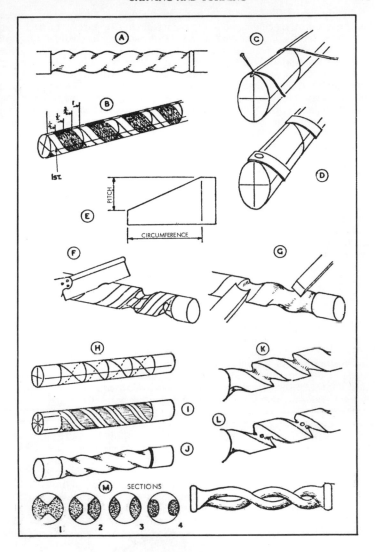

FIG. 23

represent the width of the twist in the first shaping. They start a quarter of the circumference each side of the first line. The part to be hollowed lies between these lines and is best scribbled on to avoid confusion (Fig. 23B). This completes the marking out.

The work may be supported between centres in the lathe for carving. If it is parallel and without enlarged ends, it can be held in a padded vice or preferably, in the trough suggested for fluting (Fig. 23C). The method of removing the bulk of the waste is governed by the size of the job and the available tools. A tenon or dovetail saw can be used for the first roughing out. The object is to cut a V-shaped groove around the leg. This is done by holding the saw at an angle and cutting one side of the groove while slowly revolving the work with the other hand (Fig. 23F). This is repeated with the other side of the groove so that the waste falls out. Alternatively, use a V tool, preferably a 90° one. This must be used in stages and kept very sharp, as one side will be cutting into the grain and may split the wood if used harshly. It is safest to take successive cuts heavier on the side with the grain and reverse the tool to cut the other side of the groove.

With the bulk of the waste removed further efforts are concentrated on obtaining the right shape. The bottom of the groove is cut to an even depth and shape with a fairly deep gouge, so that there is no risk of its corners digging in. Depth should be watched, as it is easy to overdo the hollowing at this stage. A chisel or flat gouge is used to round the top of the curve (Fig. 23G). Watch the apex pencil line to see that the shape is even.

A rasp or file is permissible in getting the bottom of the groove true. This can be used in one hand while the work is rotated with the other. Glasspaper is used to even the external curve.

A double or treble twist is worked in the same way, only differing in the method of marking out. Although the pitch may remain about the same as the diameter, the "lead" (the distance travelled by each spiral in a complete turn) is doubled or trebled. Consequently each twist is steeper, and the pitch can be reduced if desired.

To mark out a double twist, start with four lines lengthwise and rings at the pitch spacing, as for the single twist. Draw two spirals, by any of the methods already described, starting at opposite sides, and each making a complete circuit at two-pitch intervals (Fig. 23H). Mark points one-eighth circumference each side of these lines and draw in spirals to indicate the width of each twist (Fig. 23I). Scribble on the waste. From this point the work is the same as for a single twist. The double twist has a more delicate appearance without sacrificing strength, due to the narrower "bines" and their finer angle (Fig. 23J). A treble twist involves dividing the circumference into six, and making circuits at three-pitch intervals.

A step further, making an interesting exercise for the carver, is the separating of the two bines of the double twist. Even more tricky is the separating of the parts of a treble twist, but that should be left until experience has been gained on a double one. Open twist legs can be made of sufficient strength for light tables, but they are probably more effective as candlesticks or lamp stands, or as mirror supports on a dressing table, or similar pedestal type purpose.

An open double twist is started by marking out an ordinary double twist and removing the bulk of the waste, by the use of saw or V tool, as already described, but taking the cut rather deeper than for a closed twist (Fig. 23K). The outside can be shaped, but it is probably wiser at this stage to leave the outer part untouched, as there is less risk of damaging it by the tools forming the inside.

There are two methods of joining the two hollows. One is to drill through a large number of small holes with a morse twist drill, used in a wheel brace or an electric drill. The other is to use a veiner and carve into the bottoms of the grooves until they meet. A combination of the two may be preferred, using a few holes, as they reduce the risk of splitting, and provide a clue to the amount of wood yet to be removed by the veiner (Fig. 23L).

The best tool for cleaning out the inside is an ordinary knife blade, kept very sharp. When sufficient space has been opened, a fairly thin half-round wood file can be worked diagonally up and down the twists to even out the inequalities. When the inside is a reasonable shape, the outside is worked to shape with chisel or gouge, as before. Although the separate bines are round in section at right angles to their twist, a section straight across is elliptical (Fig. 23M). At the ends the two twists combine just before they finish and the centre should be neatly rounded.

The best way to finally remove irregularities is to use strips of glasspaper or garnet paper, pulling backwards and forwards around the bines. An abrasive with a linen backing will be more durable. Abrasives from medium down to very fine should be used in turn. Make the final strokes in the direction of the grain.

Combinations of turning and carving have been used at many times in the past. Table legs of the Tudor Period were often turned and heavily carved, mostly with conventional leaf designs (Fig. 24A). A visit to a museum or old house may show the carver many examples which he can reproduce or modify to suit his skill and ideas.

Many pieces of old furniture are splendid examples of the craftsman's skill with his tools, but they are not necessarily good examples of fitness for purpose, such as is usually demanded today. Massive bulbous legs and pillars, each covered with intricate and ornate carving, may look right in a period setting, but are unlikely to be popular with the housewife today. The wise modern carver does not let his enthusiasm for carving run away with him, and uses his form of decoration with discretion.

There have been some fine examples of combined turning and carving in the production of sets of chess men. The woods used are usually

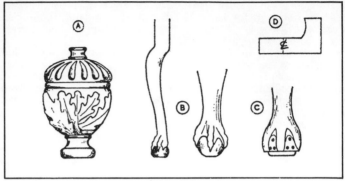

FIG. 24

boxwood (a rich yellow colour) and ebony (which is almost black). Both of these woods are much harder than those used for larger carvings. The grain is very close and not usually apparent. Tools will have to be sharpened frequently and the waste removed in small chips. Carving this harder material is quite pleasant, once the rather different technique has been grasped. In the simplest designs the only piece needing much carving is the knight, with its horse's head. This offers scope for initiative. There are many conventionalized designs in which the effect of a horse's head is obtained with quite a few tool cuts. At the other extreme are most lifelike miniatures.

Queen Anne and cabriole legs can have their feet turned before being shaped by carving. Turning gives a good guide to the general shape, removing the bulk of the waste and leaving a uniform outline as a starting point. The rest of the leg has to be shaped by normal wood-working methods. The foot is usually in the form of a three-toed claw, holding a ball (Fig. 24B). The lathe cannot give any help in shaping the ball, except that if the recesses are kept the same depth from the outside the ball must be circular. As a guide to depth, holes may be drilled in the waste portion (Fig. 24C), using a morse twist drill, or other drill without a spur, fitted with a depth stop. The holes should be slightly less than the finished depth to avoid marking what will be the finished surface. A card template (Fig. 24D) will be a guide in final shaping.

CHAPTER X

APPLICATIONS OF CARVINGS

CARVING as a means of decoration is one of the oldest arts. Wood whittled to shape with primitive tools, was a very early form of decoration, probably before painting, and certainly before men built houses or made furniture. While wood does not usually survive undamaged over thousands of years, carvings in bone and ivory have been found, dating from the earliest days, and these must have been preceded by similar work in wood.

The work of carvers and sculptors in the first place was a means of self-expression, interpreting things around in wood or stone—an art, with little or no thought for practical uses. However, society has found ways of using the work of these artists, beautifying homes and other buildings, both in their structure and furnishings; leaving us a heritage of artistry and craftsmanship.

In more recent times the work of the artist has not found so many uses. Buildings and furniture are far more strictly utilitarian. Broad plain expanses do not lend themselves so readily to embellishment. Carving, in the form of elaborate work covering almost the whole surface of an article, has fallen from favour. While intricate and extensive carving still has some place in ecclesiastical work, it is "out of fashion" for domestic use. The modern carver must have regard to this. His work is most likely to be appreciated if he applies it with restraint. He can, particularly if he is an amateur carving merely as a hobby, follow what style he likes, doing work in a bygone style, or carving in any way he fancies. If his interest is in sculpture he can use his skill to interpret life as he sees it.

In preparing a design for carving a number of points have to be borne in mind if a harmonious effect is to be produced. The carved design must be considered in relation to the article on which it is to be worked, both in appearance and in regard to the use to which it is to be put. The proportions of the design must be assessed in relation to the proportions of the article as a whole. Personal judgment and taste comes into it. A mass of tiny carvings is a waste of time and the effect is trivial. At the other extreme large and heavy carving may make the object appear overloaded with decoration. Main lines can be pencilled in on the wood or on a full-size drawing, and something of the final effect visualized.

In modern design an excess of carving is to be avoided. Good carving, applied with restraint, is the best treatment for furniture. This will usually take the form of borders or edges, with occasional small panels. The shape of panels affects the design. A square panel does not look as well as one that is about half as long one way as the other. If length is to be emphasised there should be prominent lines in the design going lengthwise, while if they go the other way the apparent breadth will be increased.

When sketching in a design, watch that the overall effect is even and balanced. In foliage, for instance, there is no need for any two leaves to be exactly alike, but they should be arranged so as to fill the area with fairly uniform spacings between. In general, there should not be large areas of unbroken background, but at the same time it is wrong to introduce unnatural forms simply because of the desire to fill space.

The best way to study designing is to examine other people's work and to pay close attention to forms which are found pleasing. Examples can be found in museums and in books. Even the excessively ornate work of many past generations can suggest an idea for a modern design, based on some part of the original. Churches can also provide work to study, particularly for the carver looking for examples in the solid.

There is nothing wrong with reproducing a design already used. Much carving is conventional and based on traditional patterns which have been found satisfactory. Usually, however, the shape and proportions of the original do not suit the work in hand. If the size is to be altered, but the proportion is to remain the same, the simplest way to re-draw the design is to use squares in the correct proportion. If, for example, the size is to be increased by half—the original is covered with $\frac{1}{4}$ in. squares and the new drawing is based on $\frac{3}{8}$ in. squares. The contents of each square is copied in turn, but it will, of course, be half as big again (Fig. 25A). If the proportion has to be altered as well, some of the work will have to depend on freehand judgment, but squares can be used again as a guide. On the original they will be squares, but on the new drawing they will be altered in the same proportion as the overall size. As a simple example, a square original panel which is to be reproduced the same width but one and a half times as long, could have the original covered with $\frac{1}{4}$ in. squares which are redrawn on $\frac{1}{4}$ in. $\times \frac{3}{8}$ in. oblongs (Fig. 25B). Borders consisting of repeated designs can be redrawn to other proportions by altering the sizes of the oblong containing the basic pattern.

Many amateur carvers will be seeking to use carving in conjunction with their other activities in wood—cabinetmaking, turning, boatbuilding etc. In a world where industry generally tends to make workmen specialists in one small part of the whole, few people, in the course of their livelihood are able to feel the satisfaction of a job well done. Fortunate is the amateur craftsman who sees a job grow from the rough wood to a finished piece, knowing that every stage in its design and construction is his. There is no such enduring satisfaction as the immense pleasure which comes from the making of something, and the carver will appreciate this, as an artist as well as a craftsman.

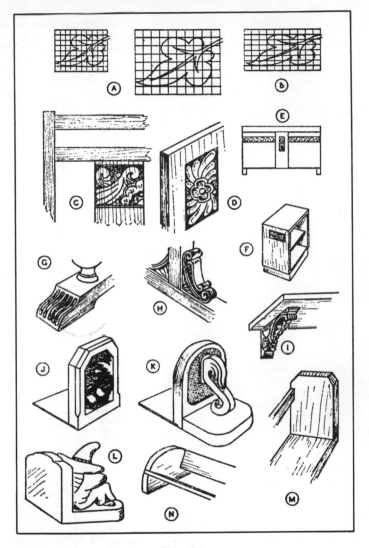

FIG. 25

What the carver does, is his concern. Carving is not only a craft in copying others' designs. Other people's work may suggest schemes to him, but he will follow his own bent, and even if he starts by thinking himself no artist, he will begin to work out designs for himself. Such is progress. A book can only point the way.

The earlier chapters of this book contain many suggestions for applying carving. This chapter suggests several more. In preparing a design the carver should always make sure that the idea is applicable to wood. Something more suitable, say, for marble, will be difficult to do and will never look right. If it is an item of furniture, be careful of overburdening it with carving.

We have passed through a period when stark simplicity, with fitness for purpose as the sole criterion, has been the fashion. This is an extreme condition in contrast to the over-ornate work at the beginning of the century. There is bound to be a swing back from this, and carving can do much to relieve the plainness of household furniture. Chair backs usually have a central panel, which is one place for carving (Fig. 25C). Doors of cabinets and sideboards have been plain, relying only on the beauty of the grain for decoration. They can often be improved by a panel (Fig. 25D), corner decorations (Fig. 17C), or by strips of carving (Fig. 25E).

When making an item of furniture which includes carving, the point at which the carving is to be done must be considered. Carving does not usually take kindly to being squeezed in a vice or knocked on the bench. Most constructional work should be done, or prepared before the carving is started. At the same time, carving is most easily done while the piece of wood is flat and unattached to other parts. Normally, the piece of wood should be prepared to size and all joints cut, but not fixed before the carving is started. The part to be carved can then be clamped to the bench and worked on in the most convenient way.

All carving should be done with a purpose. Normally the carved work is part of some structure or item of furniture, but the amateur feeling his way will produce a number of practice pieces which are merely blocks of wood, not specifically intended for any job. Where the carving has been completed successfully, some use for the block may have to be thought of. A carving cannot be hung on the wall like a picture—it should form part of something useful. Several ideas will be found amongst the following applications.

Much detail work on furniture can be done with carving tools. Edge decorations for shelves etc., have been mentioned already. A plain cabinet end may have a carved panel (Fig. 25F). This may be quite simple in low relief, or quite complex, depending on the carver's ability and the purpose of the piece.

Fluting can improve parts of furniture, as in the foot of a sideboard (Fig. 25G). Brackets, whether supporting the legs of refectory tables (Fig. 25H) or as consoles supporting a canopy over a door (Fig. 25I)

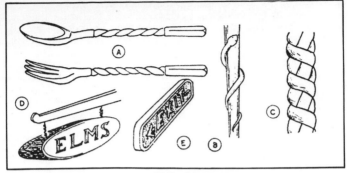

FIG. 26

can be improved by carving. This may be fluting or scrollwork, conventional leaf forms can be used, or the end finished with a mask or gargoyle, as appropriate.

Twist has been mentioned for legs, lamp standards and candlesticks. The same idea can be developed for other things. A pair of salad servers (Fig. 26A) provide a light carving project. A white wood, such as sycamore, is most appropriate. A small twist can be marked out as described for the legs, but after a little experience, much can be done by eye. The same technique can be adapted to make a snake coiled around a staff or walking stick (Fig. 26B). A little extra thickness must be left in turning for cutting the head. Twists in opposite directions can be worked. If they have the same angle of slope the result will be a series of diamonds. One twist can appear to overlap the other (Fig. 26C). Staffs for ceremonial use offer scope for twist carving.

Trays and picture frames can be improved by carved corners. Carving should not be deep or elaborate. The great expanse of a tray should be left plain, but the corners may have Gothic or other conventional leaf decorations carved (Fig. 17C). The four corners need not necessarily be the same, although the general effect should be balanced. This is one outlet for the beginner who has mastered the carving of simple leaf forms. Another thing within his scope is the carving of pieces to cover the mitres of picture frames. The modern fashion is for picture frames to be severely plain, but there are occasions when a simple carving covering the mitre at each corner will improve the appearance.

House name boards can be carved. Incised lettering, of a good style, on a plain oak board, has already been mentioned. This is dignified and smart. For a country house, or rural surroundings, the same sort of thing can be done on a slice cut diagonally across a log (Fig. 26D). The slice should be at a long angle, otherwise the grain may prove difficult in places. However, in this type of sign slight errors are not so noticeable as in more formal work. The lettering may be less formal in any case.

Name boards in relief (Fig. 26E) are also appropriate to houses and gardens, often more in keeping with their surroundings than severe painted signs. The name may suggest some original outline, as in inn signs. The carver looking for a commercial outlet for his skill, might consider the production of signs of all sorts for cafes, gardens and other outdoor purposes.

Book ends can be made up from almost any example of carving. A flat panel may have a metal base fitted (Fig. 25J), to go under the end books. A pierced bracket or something of that type can be fixed at right angles to the book ends (Fig. 25K). This pattern of book end can have a carving in the round mounted on it. Elephants or other animals pushing against the books look effective, or a whittled figure can fill the angle (Fig. 25L).

Two carved panels can be linked by a back and base to support a row of books, either upright (Fig. 25M), or as a trough with semicircular or other shaped ends (Fig. 25N).

Single panels can be made into stands for teapots, etc., although the carving will only be visible when the stand is out of use. The comparatively shallow regular form of chip carving is more appropriate for this than deep relief work. Stool tops, either shaped or rectangular, are another outlet for practice panels. Practice strip and edge decorations can be worked into the rails and legs of the stool (Fig. 6 and 7).

In the case of a number of similar practice panels, such as the output of a class of student carvers, the specimen blocks can all be of a standard size, then they can be worked into framing to form a frieze or section

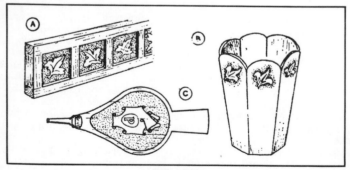

FIG. 27

of wall panelling (Fig. 27A). In the workshop this will serve as a reminder of early efforts, and add a touch of appropriate decoration.

Rectangular carvings can be built into boxes, either as lids or sides. The lid may hinge or lift off, and the purpose of the box will depend on its shape and size. Several variations on the box are possible. Several similar pieces can be linked up to make a waste paper basket or plant pot container (Fig. 27B).

Bellows have almost ceased to have a utilitarian purpose, but many people use them as decorations, and they provide an excuse for tackling carving in some traditional form, possibly more complex than would be justified on a piece of modern furniture. The heart shape of the bellows front is a convenient setting for carving of most types (Fig. 27C).

FINISHING

Where a piece of carving is part of some larger structure, a piece of furniture, or general decoration, it will usually have to receive the same finishing treatment as the rest of the work, whether the finish is the best for the carving or not. Carving does not take kindly to the high gloss finishes and does not look right under a brilliant glaze. The best appearance is when something has been done to enhance the natural colour of the wood, with a dull gloss or "egg-shell" finish.

Newly carved work may be considered to have an attractive appearance without any finishing treatment, but if nothing is done to it, dirt will enter the pores and the work will be disfigured in a way which cannot be rectified. It is therefore important that some sort of surface treatment should be given, if only to close the pores against the entry of dirt.

Staining may be done with water, spirit or oil stains. The aim should be to deepen or emphasise the natural colour of the wood, or to match it with some other part of the work, without obscuring the grain. The same stain applied to carving and to the plain wood usually appears darker on the carved surface, which may be acceptable, but if the two parts should look the same, the stain can be diluted slightly for the carving. It is wrong, as a rule, to change the colour of the wood. An exception is American whitewood, or basswood, which is almost indistinguishable from mahogany when appropriately stained.

Water stains are usually bought as powders or crystals, which are dissolved in water as required. Vandyke crystals are a cheap form of brown water stain. Water stain is cheap and covers well, but it does not penetrate the wood. Spirit stains dry quickly and penetrate well, but are not so easy to apply evenly. Some proprietary stains based on various oils, sometimes sold as "wood dyes", provide a more intense colouring. Another advantage is that after applying with a brush, they can be rubbed over with a cloth to even or lighten the colour. In this way, parts of the carving can be high-lighted to give them more prominence.

French polishing is a popular finish for furniture. An important part of the process is rubbing. The polish is made of shellac dissolved in methylated spirit, and the rubbing spreads the polish evenly while encouraging the evaporation of the spirit. This can only be done on a flat or even surface. If carving is to be part of a french-polished article, the carving should be given one or two coats of polish with a brush. Most of this will soak in, closing the pores, and leaving a dull gloss on the surface.

Many woods, particularly oak and walnut, look well if oiled. This is a rather slow process, but the results justify the time. Raw linseed oil is spread over the surface and left to soak in for several hours. The surplus is wiped off and the surface left to dry. The treatment is repeated, maybe half-a-dozen times. Linseed oil takes several days to dry. Drying may be hastened by mixing turpentine with the oil, about one part in three. After the oil has dried it can be rubbed with a coarse cloth to produce a dull gloss.

Carving may have a waxed finish. This is done with beeswax or one of the prepared furniture waxes, such as Johnson or Ronuk. A polish can be made by dissolving shredded beeswax in spirits of turpentine, then adding a little boiled oil. The wax should be well rubbed into the carving. Successive coats at intervals will bring out a rich dull gloss.

Waxing may be done as the only process, starting with the bare wood, or it can follow treatment with linseed oil. Linseed oil treatment can also be followed by french polish, but wax and french polish should not be mixed. Much commercially-produced furniture is sprayed with cellulose. This gives a high gloss which wears well and is impervious to many liquids which mark the older polishes. The shine is too bright for carving, but it may have to be accepted as an all-over treatment of a piece of furniture. It is not really in keeping with the spirit of carving, and is best avoided.

Varnish usually has no place on carved work—except on exterior work. It is essential on boat work—figure heads, name boards etc. Varnish stain is a cheap finish for floors, but it would only be regarded as shoddy on carving.

GLOSSARY

Acanthus leaf	Conventional leaf form, based on Greek original.
American whitewood	Soft yellow wood, obtainable in wide boards.
Arkansas	Type of sharpening stone.
Arris	Sharp edge.
Ash	Strong coarse hard wood, unsuitable for carving, but used for tool handles.
Basswood	Alternative name for American whitewood.
Bead	Curved ridge.
Beech	Close-grained moderately hard wood, used for mallets and planes.
Bine	A part of a twist turning.
Birch	Brown moderately hard wood.
Bosting in	Roughing a carving to shape by chopping away the bulk of the waste wood.
Cabriole leg	Originally a goat's leg, but now a type of table or chair leg with an animal or bird foot.
Carborundum	Type of sharpening stone.
Cartouche	Type of centre piece, usually carrying a monogram, originating in the rolled edge effect of parchment.
Carver's bench screw	Screw with tapered end for screwing into work, and bolt end with wing nut for fixing to bench.
Chamfer	Bevel.
Chase carving	Outlining design with gouge.
Chip carving	Knife-cut triangular-recessed carving.
Chisel	Cutting tool with a flat section.
—bent or spoon	Curved end.
—corner or screw	With cutting edge at an angle.
—dog-legged	Cranked with a double angle.
—fish-tailed	Small blade on long shaft.
—spade	Alternative name to fish-tailed.
—square	With cutting edge at right angles to tool.
Cleated	Rounded, particularly the angle at the bottom of a V tool.
Concave	Inside of a curve.
Console	Bracket under a canopy.
Conventional design	Plant form or other natural shape adapted to suit the requirements of the material.
Convex	Outside of a curve.
Dog	Clip for cramping work to bench.
Dog-legged	Tool cranked with a double bend to off-set the cutting edge.
Ebony	Very hard black wood.
Empire hardwoods	Collective name for many post-war timbers from the Commonwealth.
Eye	Carved hole, giving a dark shadow.

83

Facet	Small flat surface.
Festoon	Alternative name for swag.
Flushing	Tearing out grain.
Fluter	Small gouge with quick curve.
Fluting	Grooving.
Fuming	Colouring wood by exposing to ammonia fumes.
Gothic	A period in architecture.
Gouge	A cutting tool with a curved cross-section.
—*back bent*	With the end curved downwards.
—*bent*	With a curve upwards lengthwise.
—*fish-tail*	With a small blade on a long shaft.
—*flat*	With a very shallow curve.
—*front bent*	With the end curved upwards.
—*quick*	With a deep curve.
—*spade*	Alternative name to fish-tailed.
—*spoon-bit*	Alternative name to front bent.
Grounding tool	A front-bent gouge or chisel.
Holdfast	A cramping device which has a leg passing through a hole in the bench.
Incised work	Design cut in outline.
India	Type of sharpening stone.
In the round	Solid carving in three dimensions.
Jarrah	Hard red wood, suitable for exterior work.
Jig	Holding or marking-out device.
Leg cramp	Alternative name to holdfast.
Lignum Vitae	Very hard and heavy wood.
Lime	Soft, light, easily-cut wood.
Linenfold	Carving based on folds of cloth.
Liverpool knife	A carving knife with a long bent blade.
Lobe	Projecting end of the part of a leaf.
London knife	A carving knife with a short bent blade.
Long pod	Spade tool with a blade longer than usual.
Macaroni tool	Gouge-type tool with angular U section.
Mahogany	Red-brown moderately hard wood.
Modelling	Carving in deep relief.
Naturalesque	Carved to appear as like the natural thing as possible.
Obechi, or Obeche	Smooth yellow wood, unsuitable for carving.
Ogee	Double curve moulding section.
Oak	Tough, hardwood, popular for carving.
Parting tool	Alternative name to V tool.
Patera	Circular piece of ornament.
Pear	Clean-cutting wood.
Pierced	Cut right through.
Pilaster	A rectangular column.
Pine	Soft wood, good for practise carving.
Pipe	Tube effect due to close fold of leaf, linen, etc.
Pitch	Distance from top of one thread to the top of the next on a screw or twist turning.
Pitting	Damaged tools, caused by rust.
Plane	Light brown hard wood.
Rasp	A type of file with individually-cut teeth.

Rebate, or rabbet	A recessed edge.
Reeding	Raised curved-section bars.
Relief	Standing out from background.
Renaissance	Period in architecture.
Riffler	A small file on a long handle, for filing in recesses.
Scalloping	Alternative name to reeding.
Scratch stock	Tool for scraping beads and other moulded forms.
Scroll	Parchment or streamer form.
Serif	Pointed ends of letters.
Setting-in	Cutting down the outline of a design.
Shake	Natural crack.
Sinking	Recessing the background so that the design stands out in relief.
Slip	A shaped oilstone for the insides of gouges and V tools.
Sloyd knife	A type of general-purpose knife.
Stippled	Dotted.
Strop	Leather dressed with fine abrasive for sharpening tools.
Swag	Hanging cluster.
Sweep	The curve of a gouge.
Sycamore	Hard white wood.
Teak	Strong brown hard wood, suitable for exterior work.
Threading-in	Roughening background with a V tool.
Tracery	Openwork decoration.
Trefoil	Spray of three leaves, etc.
Tudor	Historical period.
Twist turning	Carved screw effect.
Undercut	The edge cut at an angle under the design.
Veiner	Small quick gouge.
V tool	A double-sided chisel cutting a V-shaped groove.
curved	With the blade curved upwards.
—spoon bit	With the end curved upwards, for cutting in recesses.
Wagon bevelling	Chamferred edges, not reaching the ends of the wood.
Walnut	Dark brown hardwood.
Washita	Type of sharpening stone.
Yellow Pine	Good quality soft wood.

LONDON PATTERN CARVING TOOLS

M 1 Square Chisel
Sizes: $\frac{1}{4}$, $\frac{3}{8}$, $\frac{1}{2}$ in.

M 2 Skew Chisel
Sizes: $\frac{1}{4}$, $\frac{3}{8}$, $\frac{1}{2}$ in.

M 21 Spoon-bit Chisel, Square
Sizes: $\frac{1}{8}$, $\frac{1}{4}$ in.

M 47 Veiner
Sizes: $\frac{1}{16}$ in.

LONDON PATTERN CARVING TOOLS—(cont.)

M 3 to 11 Straight Gouge
M 3, 8, 11—Sizes: $\frac{1}{8}$, $\frac{1}{4}$, $\frac{3}{8}$, $\frac{1}{2}$ in.
M 5, 6, 7—Sizes: $\frac{1}{8}$, $\frac{1}{4}$, $\frac{3}{8}$, $\frac{1}{2}$, $\frac{5}{8}$ in.

Curved Gouge
M 14—Sizes: $\frac{1}{4}$, $\frac{3}{8}$, $\frac{1}{2}$, $\frac{5}{8}$ in.
M 16—Sizes: $\frac{1}{8}$, $\frac{1}{4}$, $\frac{3}{8}$, $\frac{1}{2}$, $\frac{5}{8}$ in.

M 39 Straight V Parting Tool
Sizes: $\frac{1}{8}$, $\frac{1}{4}$, $\frac{3}{8}$, $\frac{1}{2}$ in.

M 40 Curved V Parting Tool
Sizes: $\frac{1}{4}$, $\frac{1}{2}$ in.

M 153
SET OF SIX
SMALL SIZE
CARVING TOOLS
(Length 6½ in. overall)
Comprises:
1 Square Chisel $\frac{5}{16}$ in.
1 Skew Chisel $\frac{5}{16}$ in.
1 Bent Square Chisel, $\frac{5}{16}$ in.
1 Bent Gouge, $\frac{5}{16}$ in.
1 Straight Gouge, $\frac{3}{16}$ in.
1 Bent V Tool, $\frac{3}{16}$ in.

M 153

M 277
Wood Carvers screws
8 x $\frac{3}{8}$ in.

M 204
Beechwood Mallets
4 in. diameter approx.

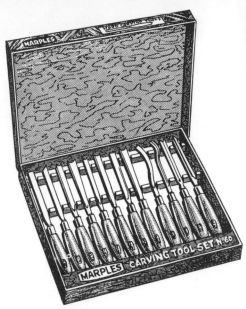

M 60
SET OF TWELVE,
FULL SIZE
Comprises:
(Length $9\frac{1}{2}$ in. overall)
No.
  1 Square Chisel, $\frac{1}{2}$ in.
  2 Skew Chisel, $\frac{1}{4}$ in.
  5 Straight Carving
    Gouge, $\frac{1}{2}$, $\frac{5}{8}$ in.
  6 Straight Carving
    Gouge, $\frac{1}{8}$, $\frac{3}{8}$ in.
  7 Straight Carving
    Gouge, $\frac{1}{4}$ in.
  8 Straight Carving
    Gouge, $\frac{1}{2}$ in.
 14 Bent Gouge, $\frac{1}{4}$ in.
 21 Spoon-bit Chisel, $\frac{1}{8}$ in.
 39 V Parting Tool, $\frac{1}{4}$ in.
 47 Veiner, $\frac{1}{16}$ in.
Complete with Slip
  Stone.

M 152

M 152
SET OF SIX
MEDIUM SIZE
(Length 8 in. overall)
Comprises:
1 Skew Chisel, $\frac{1}{4}$ in.
1 Straight Gouge, $\frac{3}{8}$ in.
1 Straight Gouge, $\frac{1}{2}$ in.
1 Bent Gouge, $\frac{1}{4}$ in.
1 Spoon-bit Chisel, $\frac{1}{8}$ in.
1 V Tool, $\frac{5}{16}$ in.
  Sharpening Stone